W9-CEA-705

cupcakes & muffins

First published in 2010
LOVE FOOD is an imprint of Parragon Books Ltd

Parragon
Queen Street House
4 Queen Street
Bath BA1 1HE, UK

ISBN: 978-1-4075-9090-5
Printed in China

Created and produced by Ivy Contract

Photography: Sian Irvine
Food styling by Jack Sargeson, Anna Irvine, and Maud Eden
New recipes by Susanna Tee with Sarah Banbery, and Jacqueline Bellefontaine

Notes for the Reader
This book uses imperial, metric, and US cup measurements. Follow the same units of measurement throughout; do not mix imperial and metric. All spoon measurements are level: teaspoons are assumed to be 5 ml, and tablespoons are assumed to be 15 ml. Unless otherwise stated, milk is assumed to be whole, eggs and individual vegetables, such as potatoes, are medium, and pepper is freshly ground black pepper.

The times given are an approximate guide only. Preparation times differ according to the techniques used by different people and the cooking times may also vary from those given. Optional ingredients, variations, or serving suggestions have not been included in the calculations.

Recipes using raw or very lightly cooked eggs should be avoided by infants, the elderly, pregnant women, convalescents, and anyone suffering from an illness. Pregnant and breastfeeding women are advised to avoid eating peanuts and peanut products. Sufferers from nut allergies should be aware that some of the ready-made ingredients used in the recipes in this book may contain nuts. Always check the packaging before use.

cupcakes & muffins

200 inspirational cupcake & muffin recipes

CONSULTANT EDITOR: **Susanna Tee**

Contents

Introduction

The cupcakes and muffins included in this book are easy and enjoyable to make, fun to eat, and great to share whatever the time of day. They are the perfect choice for a mid-morning coffee or afternoon tea, at a children's party, or on a festive occasion. Whatever the reason, you are sure to find what you are looking for among the delicious goodies that have been gathered together in this collection.

The star ingredients

Sugar, fat, eggs, flour, and a liquid are the basic ingredients that the majority of the recipes share.

Sugar

Superfine sugar is usually recommended because it dissolves more easily than granulated sugar. Nevertheless, granulated sugar can be used if necessary.

Fat

Butter is the fat that is suggested in most of the recipes, as this adds richness and gives the best flavor. However, margarine can be used as an alternative, and is less expensive. It is important, though, to use a margarine containing not less than 60 percent fat; choose a hard margarine that is described on the packet as suitable for baking. The exception is when a recipe calls for a soft margarine. In this instance all the ingredients are beaten together with an electric mixer until mixed.

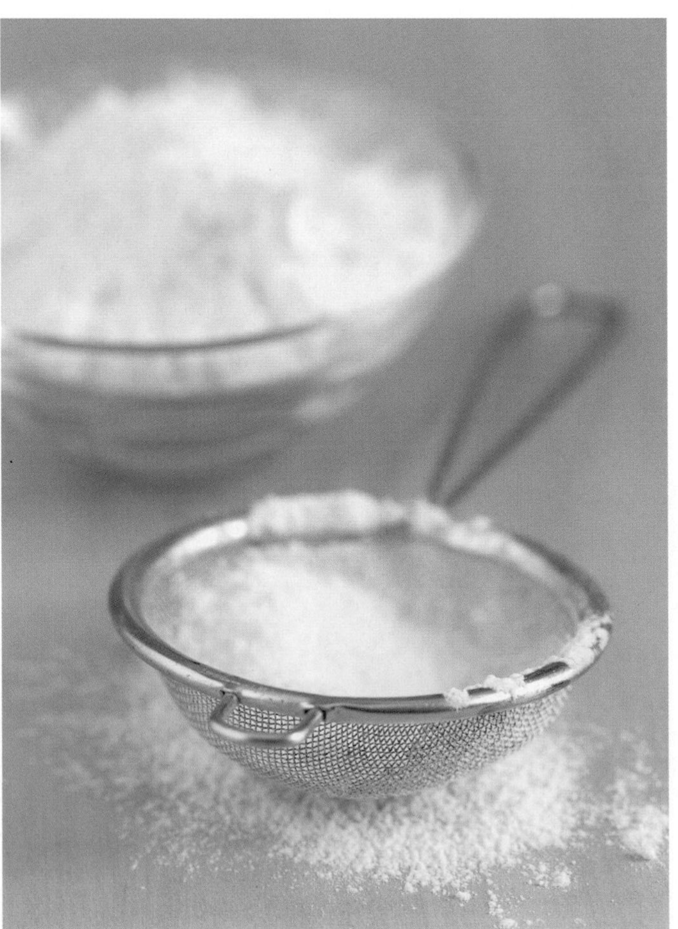

Eggs

The size of eggs used in the recipes is medium unless otherwise stated. If possible, use eggs that are at room temperature because cold eggs can cause the mixture to curdle and will result in a less soft mixture.

Flour

The flour used in the recipes may be all-purpose or self-rising. Should you need self-rising flour but only have all-purpose, sift 2½ teaspoons of baking powder into every 8 oz/225 g all-purpose flour.

Liquid

The liquid in the recipes is used to bind the ingredients together and is usually milk, eggs, butter, oil, water, or fruit juice.

Assuring success

Almost all the recipes in the book are easy to make. Follow these useful suggestions and you will be guaranteed success every time you bake:

- Preheat the oven for 10–15 minutes before baking, even if the oven manufacturer's instructions suggest that this is not necessary. If you have a fan-assisted oven, reduce the temperature according to their instructions.
- It is important that ingredients are measured accurately, so it is worth investing in good quality measuring cups and standard measuring spoons.
- Get into the habit of preparing paper liners and pans before commencing preparation, as mixtures that contain self-rising flour start to activate once the liquid has been added to them and should therefore be baked as soon as possible after they have been prepared.
- It is not necessary to sift flour unless you are combining several dry ingredients to facilitate even mixing.
- When butter or hard margarine needs to be softened before blending with another ingredient, either remove it from the refrigerator and leave at room temperature for about 1 hour, or cut into cubes, place in a bowl, and microwave on High for 10 seconds, until softened slightly. Be careful not to allow it to melt.
- After adding the flour to a mixture, do not overbeat it as this will make the mixture tough.
- Position baking trays on the middle rack of the oven for even browning.
- Unless otherwise stated, transfer cupcakes and muffins to a wire rack directly after they are removed from the oven, and leave to cool. This will allow the steam to evaporate and prevent them from becoming soggy.
- When baking, try to resist the temptation to open the oven door during the first half of the cooking time as cold air can cause the mixture to sink in the middle.

Equipment & helpful techniques

Making any of the recipes in this book requires very little special equipment and, in many cases, improvisation can be helpful! Nevertheless, here are some suggestions that you may find useful:

- If a recipe asks for toasted nuts and you do not have any, you can toast them yourself. Preheat the oven to 350°F/180°C. Spread the nuts in a single layer on a baking sheet and cook in the preheated oven for 5–10 minutes, turning and watching them carefully until golden brown.
- Many of the recipes require you to melt chocolate in a heatproof bowl set over a saucepan of simmering water. This is the safest way to melt it because it will not overheat and become dry. Make sure the bowl does not touch the water. You can also melt chocolate in a microwave. To do this, break the chocolate into a heatproof bowl and cook on Low until the chocolate is soft on top. As a guide, 3½ oz/100 g will take about 4 minutes. Check and stir every minute.
- With a few exceptions, most of the recipes in this book will keep well in a tin or airtight container.
- Ideally, store baked cupcakes and muffins undecorated. Any item that is decorated with cream, cream cheese, or yogurt should be stored in the refrigerator.
- Most cupcakes and muffins can be frozen and thawed at short notice, but most are best when just baked.

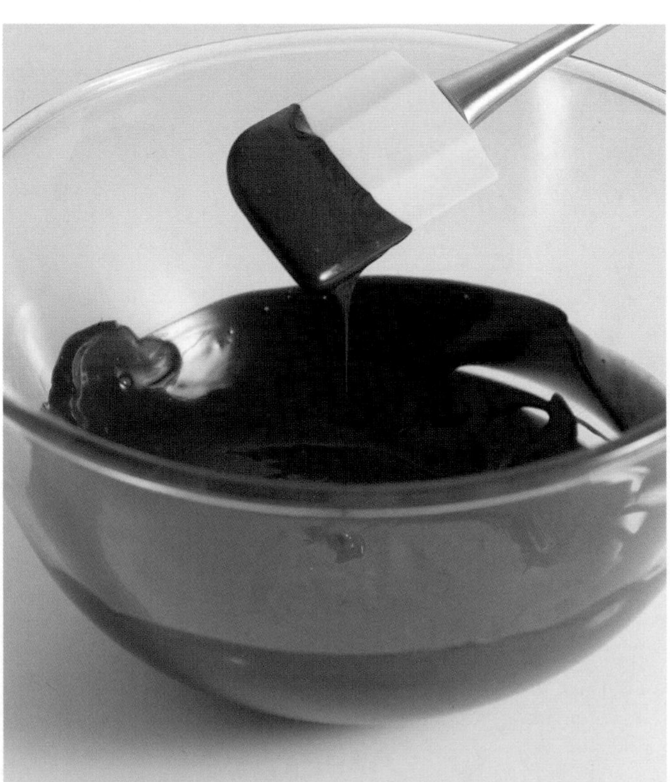

The finishing touches

Basic icing

1 cup confectioners' sugar
1 tbsp cold water

Sift the sugar into a bowl and gradually add the water, then beat together until the icing coats the back of a spoon.

American frosting

1⅛ cups superfine sugar
4 tbsp water
¼ tsp cream of tartar
½ tsp vanilla extract
1 large egg white

Place the sugar, water, and cream of tartar into a saucepan and heat gently until the sugar has dissolved. Add the vanilla and heat (without boiling), stirring until the temperature reads 250°F/120°C on a sugar thermometer. Let cool slightly. Whisk the egg white in a large bowl until stiff, then continue whisking as you add the syrup in a thin stream and until it is smooth and thick.

Chocolate frosting

3½ oz/100 g semisweet chocolate, chopped
scant ⅔ cup butter, softened
1¼ cups confectioners' sugar
½ tsp chocolate extract

Place the chocolate in a heatproof bowl, set the bowl over a saucepan of gently simmering water until melted. Let cool. Beat the butter in a bowl until fluffy, then sift in the sugar and beat until smooth. Add the cooled chocolate and chocolate extract and beat until combined.

Buttercream

1 cup butter, softened
1 tbsp cream or milk
3 cups confectioners' sugar
Note *To make chocolate buttercream, substitute ½ cup cocoa for sugar*

Place the butter and cream in a bowl and beat together. Gradually sift in the confectioners' sugar and beat until smooth.

Fondant

4 ⅓ cups confectioners' sugar
1 large egg white
2 tbsp liquid glycerin
1 tsp vanilla extract or almond extract

Sift the confectioners' sugar into a large bowl and gradually beat in the egg white until the mixture is thick and smooth. Beat in the glycerin and vanilla extract.

Cream cheese frosting

9 tbsp butter, softened
1 cup cream cheese
scant 4 cups confectioners' sugar
1 tsp vanilla extract

Place the butter and cheese in a bowl and beat until light and fluffy. Gradually sift in the sugar, add the vanilla, and beat until smooth.

01 *Iced cupcakes*

MAKES 16

8 tbsp butter, softened
½ cup superfine sugar
2 eggs, lightly beaten
heaping ¾ cup self-rising flour

TOPPING
1¾ cups confectioners' sugar
about 2 tbsp warm water
a few drops of food coloring (optional)
sugar flowers, colored sprinkles, candied cherries, and/or chocolate strands, for decorating

Preheat the oven to 375°F/190°C. Line two 12-hole muffin pans with 16 paper liners. Place the butter and sugar in a large bowl and beat together until light and fluffy, then gradually beat in the eggs. Sift in the flour and fold into the mixture. Spoon the batter into the paper liners.

Bake in the preheated oven for 15–20 minutes. Transfer to a wire rack to cool completely.

To make the icing, sift the confectioners' sugar into a bowl and stir in just enough warm water to mix to a smooth paste that is thick enough to coat the back of a wooden spoon. Stir in a few drops of food coloring, if using, then spread the icing over the cupcakes and decorate, as liked.

02 *Orange cupcakes*

Add the grated rind of ½ orange to the cake batter after beating in the eggs. Use orange juice instead of water when making the icing.

03 *Lemon cupcakes*

Add the grated rind of ½ lemon to the cake batter after beating in the eggs. Use lemon juice instead of water when making the icing.

04 *Chocolate cupcakes*

Replace 2 tablespoons of the flour with 2 tablespoons of cocoa and add 2 teaspoons of cocoa to the confectioners' sugar when making the icing.

05 *Coffee cupcakes*

Dissolve 2 tablespoons of instant coffee in 3 tablespoons of boiling water. Add about two thirds to the cake batter after beating the eggs. Add the remainder to the confectioners' sugar when making the icing.

06 *Mocha cupcakes*

Dissolve 1 tablespoon of instant coffee in 2 tablespoons of boiling water and beat in after adding the eggs. Add 1 tablespoon of cocoa to the flour and fold in. For a mocha icing, add 1 teaspoon of cocoa to the confectioners' sugar. Dissolve 1 teaspoon of instant coffee in 1 tablespoon of boiling water and stir into the confectioners' sugar mixture with enough water until smooth.

07 *Almond cupcakes*

Add 1 teaspoon of almond extract after beating in the eggs. Replace 2 tablespoons of the flour with ground almonds.

08 *Nutty cupcakes*

Add ¼ cup finely chopped walnuts, pecans, or toasted hazelnuts before folding in the flour.

09 Candy-topped vanilla cupcakes

MAKES 18

generous 8 tbsp butter, softened, or soft margarine
¾ cup superfine sugar
1½ tsp vanilla extract
2 large eggs, lightly beaten
scant 1½ cups self-rising flour

TOPPING
1 quantity buttercream (page 8)
a selection of classic small candies, such as jelly beans, for decorating

Preheat the oven to 375°/190°C. Line two 12-hole muffin pans with 18 paper liners. Place the butter and sugar in a large bowl and beat together until light and fluffy, then beat in the vanilla extract. Gradually beat in the eggs, then sift in the flour and fold into the mixture. Spoon the batter into the paper liners.

Bake in the preheated oven for 12–15 minutes, or until golden and springy to the touch. Transfer to a wire rack to cool completely.

Place the buttercream in a pastry bag fitted with a small star tip and pipe the buttercream on top of each cake. Arrange the candies on top to decorate.

10 Candy-topped chocolate cupcakes

Reduce the vanilla extract to ½ teaspoon. Melt 2½ oz/70 g semisweet chocolate, broken into pieces, and stir into the cake batter after beating in the eggs. Decorate with chocolate buttercream (page 8) and small chocolate candies.

11 Birthday party cakes

MAKES 24

1 cup butter, softened, or soft margarine
heaping 1 cup superfine sugar
4 eggs
1⅔ cups self-rising flour

TOPPING
¾ cup butter, softened
3 cups confectioners' sugar
a variety of candies and chocolates, sugar-coated chocolates, dried fruits, edible sugar flower shapes, cake decorating sprinkles, silver or gold dragées, colored sprinkles, various tubes of colored decorating icing, and candles and candleholders (optional), for decorating

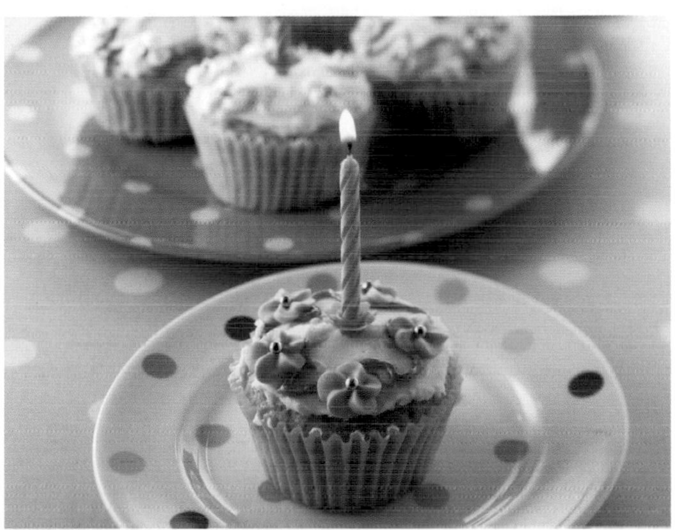

Preheat the oven to 350°F/180°C. Line two 12-hole muffin pans with 24 paper liners. Place the butter, sugar, eggs, and flour in a large bowl and beat together until just smooth. Spoon the batter into the paper liners.

Bake in the preheated oven for 15–20 minutes, or until well risen, golden brown, and firm to the touch. Transfer to a wire rack to cool.

To make the frosting, place the butter in a bowl and beat until fluffy. Sift in the confectioners' sugar and beat together until smooth. When the cakes are cold, spread the frosting on top of each cake, then decorate as you like and place a candle in the top of each, if using.

12 Citrus almond party cakes

For more grown-up party cakes, replace heaping ⅓ cup of the flour with ground almonds and fold in ¼ cup finely chopped candied peel. Decorate with sugared almonds.

13 Chocolate butterfly cakes

MAKES 12

1 oz/25 g semisweet chocolate, broken into pieces
9 tbsp butter, softened
⅔ cup superfine sugar
heaping 1 cup self-rising flour
2 large eggs
2 tbsp unsweetened cocoa
confectioners' sugar, for dusting

LEMON BUTTERCREAM
7 tbsp butter, softened
2 cups confectioners' sugar
grated rind of ½ lemon
1 tbsp lemon juice

Preheat the oven to 350°F/180°C. Line a 12-hole muffin pan with 12 paper liners. Place the chocolate in a heatproof bowl, set the bowl over a saucepan of gently simmering water, and heat until melted, then let cool slightly.

Place the butter, sugar, flour, eggs, and cocoa in a large bowl and beat together until the mixture is just smooth. Beat in the melted chocolate. Spoon the batter into the paper liners.

Bake in the preheated oven for 15 minutes, or until springy to the touch. Transfer to a wire rack to cool completely.

To make the frosting, place the butter in a bowl and beat until fluffy, then gradually sift in the confectioners' sugar and beat to combine. Beat in the lemon rind, then gradually beat in the lemon juice. Cut the top off each cake, then cut the top in half. Pipe the buttercream over the cut surface of each cake and push the 2 cut cake pieces into the frosting to form wings. Dust with sifted confectioners' sugar.

14 Chocolate orange butterfly cakes

Add the grated rind of ½ orange and 2 tablespoons of orange juice to the cake batter. For the frosting, replace the lemon juice and rind with orange juice and rind and decorate the completed cakes with very fine strips of orange rind, if liked.

15 Chocolate nut butterfly cakes

Add ¼ cup finely chopped hazelnuts to the cake batter. Sprinkle a few chopped toasted hazelnuts on the top to decorate.

16 White chocolate butterfly cakes

Replace the melted semisweet chocolate with melted white chocolate. Decorate the cakes with chocolate buttercream (page 8).

17 *Honey & spice cakes*

MAKES 24

heaping ½ cup butter
⅓ cup brown sugar
¼ cup honey
scant 1½ cups self-rising flour
1 tsp ground allspice
2 eggs, lightly beaten
24 whole blanched almonds

Preheat the oven to 350°F/180°C. Line two 12-hole muffin pans with 24 paper liners. Place the butter, sugar, and honey in a large saucepan and heat gently, stirring, until the butter is melted. Remove the pan from the heat. Sift together the flour and allspice and stir into the mixture in the saucepan, then beat in the eggs until smooth.

Spoon the batter into the paper liners and place an almond on top of each one. Bake in the preheated oven for 20–25 minutes, or until well risen and golden brown. Transfer to a wire rack to cool completely.

18 *Pecan & maple spice cakes*

Replace the honey with maple syrup and the allspice with cinnamon. Decorate each cake with a pecan instead of an almond.

19 *Nutmeg & hazelnut cakes*

Add 1 tablespoon of finely chopped toasted hazelnuts to the honey and butter mixture. Replace the allspice with nutmeg and decorate each cake with a hazelnut instead of an almond.

20 Sticky gingerbread cupcakes

MAKES 16

¾ cup all-purpose flour
2 tsp ground ginger
¾ tsp ground cinnamon
1 piece preserved ginger, finely chopped
¾ tsp baking soda
4 tbsp milk
6 tbsp butter, softened
⅓ cup dark brown sugar
2 tbsp blackstrap molasses
2 eggs, lightly beaten
1 piece preserved ginger, sliced, for decorating

FROSTING
6 tbsp butter, softened
1½ cups confectioners' sugar
2 tbsp ginger syrup from the preserved ginger jar

Preheat the oven to 325°F/160°C. Line two 12-hole muffin pans with 16 paper liners. Sift the flour, ground ginger, and cinnamon together into a bowl. Add the chopped ginger and toss in the flour mixture until it is well coated. Place the baking soda and milk in a separate bowl and stir to dissolve.

Place the butter and sugar in a large bowl and beat together until light and fluffy.

Beat in the blackstrap molasses, then gradually mix in the eggs. Beat in the flour mixture and gradually add the milk. Spoon the batter into the paper liners.

Bake in the preheated oven for 20 minutes, or until well risen and golden brown. Transfer to a wire rack to cool competely.

To make the frosting, place the butter in a bowl and beat until fluffy. Sift in the confectioners' sugar, add the ginger syrup, and beat together until smooth and creamy.

When the cupcakes are cold, spread the frosting on top of each cake, then decorate with pieces of the preserved ginger to decorate.

21 Sticky gingersnap cupcakes

Add ¼ cup finely chopped walnuts or pecans with the chopped preserved ginger. Decorate with chopped nuts.

22 Dark & white fudge cakes

MAKES 20

generous ¾ cup water
6 tbsp butter
½ cup superfine sugar
1 tbsp dark corn syrup
3 tbsp milk
1 tsp vanilla extract
1 tsp baking soda
1⅔ cups all-purpose flour
2 tbsp unsweetened cocoa

TOPPING
1¾ oz/50 g semisweet chocolate, broken into pieces
4 tbsp water
3½ tbsp butter
1¾ oz/50 g white chocolate, broken into pieces
3 cups confectioners' sugar
3½ oz/100 g semisweet chocolate shavings and 3½ oz/100 g white chocolate shavings, for decorating

Preheat the oven to 350°F/180°C. Line two 12-hole muffin pans with 20 paper liners. Place the water, butter, sugar, and syrup in a saucepan and heat gently, stirring, until the sugar has dissolved. Bring to a boil, reduce the heat, and cook gently for 5 minutes. Let cool.

Meanwhile, place the milk and vanilla extract in a bowl. Add the baking soda and stir to dissolve. Sift the flour and cocoa into a separate bowl and add the syrup mixture. Stir in the milk mixture and beat until smooth, then spoon the batter into the paper liners.

Bake in the preheated oven for 20 minutes, or until well risen and firm to the touch. Transfer to a wire rack to cool completely.

To make the frosting, place the semisweet chocolate in a small heatproof bowl, add half the water and half the butter, set the bowl over a saucepan of gently simmering water, and heat until melted. Stir until smooth and then let stand over the water. Repeat with the white chocolate and remaining water and butter. Sift half the confectioners' sugar into each bowl and beat until smooth and thick.

When the cupcakes are cold, top alternately with each frosting, then let set. Decorate with chocolate shavings.

23 Pecan fudge cupcakes

Stir ¼ cup chopped pecans into the flour and cocoa mixture before adding the syrup. Sprinkle chopped nuts instead of chocolate shavings on top of the frosting.

24 Frosted peanut butter cupcakes

MAKES 16

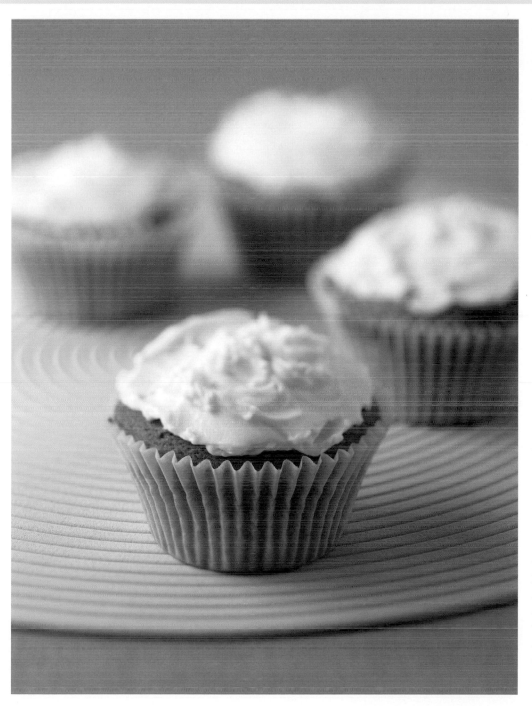

4 tbsp butter, softened,
or soft margarine
heaping 1 cup light brown sugar
½ cup crunchy peanut butter
2 eggs, lightly beaten
1 tsp vanilla extract
1⅔ cups all-purpose flour
2 tsp baking powder
generous ⅓ cup milk

FROSTING
heaping ¾ cup soft cream cheese
2 tbsp butter, softened
2 cups confectioners' sugar

Preheat the oven to 350°F/180°C. Line two 12-hole muffin pans with 16 paper liners. Place the butter, sugar, and peanut butter in a bowl and beat together for 1–2 minutes, or until well mixed. Gradually beat in the eggs, then add the vanilla extract. Sift in the flour and baking powder, then fold them into the mixture, alternating with the milk. Spoon the batter into the paper liners.

Bake in the preheated oven for 25 minutes, or until well risen and golden brown. Transfer to a wire rack to cool completely.

To make the frosting, place the cream cheese and butter in a large bowl and beat together until smooth. Sift the confectioners' sugar into the mixture, beat together until well mixed, then spread the frosting on top of each cupcake.

25 Peanut butter & jam cupcakes

Spoon half the batter into the paper liners then place about ½ teaspoon of strawberry or raspberry jam into the center of each. Carefully spoon the remaining batter into the paper liners so that it completely encloses the jam. Sprinkle with a little raw brown sugar and bake as before.

26 Chocolate peanut butter cupcakes

Spoon half the batter into the paper liners then place about ½ teaspoon of chocolate spread into the center of each. Carefully spoon the remaining batter into the paper liners so that it completely encloses the chocolate spread. Bake as before. Cool and spread with extra chocolate spread.

27 Blueberry muffins

Makes 12

6 tbsp sunflower oil or 6 tbsp butter, melted and cooled, plus extra for greasing
2 cups all-purpose flour
1 tbsp baking powder
pinch of salt
heaping ½ cup light brown sugar
heaping 1 cup frozen blueberries
2 eggs
generous 1 cup milk
1 tsp vanilla extract
finely grated rind of 1 lemon

Preheat the oven to 400°F/200°C. Grease a 12-hole muffin pan. Sift together the flour, baking powder, and salt into a large bowl. Stir in the sugar and blueberries.

Place the eggs in a large pitcher or bowl and beat lightly, then beat in the milk, oil, vanilla extract, and lemon rind. Make a well in the center of the dry ingredients and pour in the beaten liquid ingredients. Stir until just combined; do not overmix. Spoon the batter into the muffin pan.

Bake in the preheated oven for 20 minutes, or until well risen, golden brown, and firm to the touch. Let cool in the pan for 5 minutes, then serve warm or transfer to a wire rack to cool completely.

28 With white chocolate topping

Rub 3 tablespoons of butter into heaping ⅓ cup all-purpose flour until the mixture resembles breadcrumbs, then stir in 2 tablespoons of superfine sugar, 2 tablespoons of dried blueberries, and 1¾ oz/50 g grated white chocolate and scatter over the muffins before baking.

29 Blackberry & apple muffins

Makes 12

6 tbsp sunflower oil or 6 tbsp butter, melted and cooled, plus extra for greasing
2 cups all-purpose flour
1 tbsp baking powder
pinch of salt
heaping ½ cup light brown sugar
1 large apple
2 eggs
generous 1 cup buttermilk
1 tsp vanilla extract
1 cup frozen blackberries
scant ¼ cup raw brown sugar

Preheat the oven to 400°F/200°C. Grease a 12-hole muffin pan. Sift together the flour, baking powder, and salt into a large bowl. Stir in the brown sugar. Peel, core, and finely chop the apple. Add to the flour mixture and stir together.

Place the eggs in a large pitcher or bowl and beat lightly, then beat in the buttermilk, oil, and vanilla extract. Make a well in the center of the dry ingredients, pour in the beaten liquid ingredients, and add the blackberries. Stir gently until just combined; do not overmix. Spoon the batter into the muffin pan. Sprinkle the raw brown sugar over the tops of the muffins.

Bake in the preheated oven for 20 minutes, until well risen, golden brown, and firm to the touch. Let cool in the pan for 5 minutes, then serve warm or transfer to a wire rack to cool completely.

30 Mixed berry muffins

Omit the apple and replace the blackberries with 1⅓ cups mixed fresh berries.

31 *Apple streusel muffins*

MAKES 12

2 cups all-purpose flour
1 tbsp baking powder
½ tsp ground cinnamon
pinch of salt
heaping ½ cup light brown sugar
1 large apple
2 eggs
generous 1 cup milk
6 tbsp sunflower oil or 6 tbsp butter, melted and cooled

STREUSEL TOPPING
scant ½ cup all purpose flour
¼ tsp ground cinnamon
2½ tbsp butter, cut into small pieces
2 tbsp light brown sugar

Preheat the oven to 400°F/200°C. Line a 12-hole muffin pan with 12 paper liners.

To make the streusel topping, place the flour and cinnamon in a bowl. Add the butter and rub it in with your fingertips until the mixture resembles fine breadcrumbs. Stir in the sugar and set aside.

To make the muffins, sift together the flour, baking powder, cinnamon, and salt into a large bowl. Stir in the sugar. Peel, core, and finely chop the apple. Add to the flour mixture and stir together. Place the eggs in a large pitcher or bowl and beat lightly, then beat in the milk and oil.

Make a well in the center of the dry ingredients and pour in the beaten liquid ingredients. Stir gently until just combined; do not overmix. Spoon the batter into the paper liners. Scatter the streusel topping over each muffin.

Bake in the preheated oven for 20 minutes, or until well risen, golden brown, and firm to the touch. Let cool in the pan for 5 minutes, then serve warm or transfer to a wire rack to cool completely.

32 *With apple brandy butter*

Beat 1 tablespoon of apple brandy and 2 tablespoons of finely chopped dried apple into 6 tablespoons of softened butter and serve with the muffins.

33 *Apricot & banana muffins*

MAKES 12

6 tbsp sunflower oil or 6 tbsp butter, melted and cooled, plus extra for greasing
2 cups all-purpose flour
1 tbsp baking powder
pinch of salt
heaping ½ cup superfine sugar
⅓ cup dried apricots, finely chopped
2 bananas
about ⅔ cup milk
2 eggs

Preheat the oven to 400°F/200°C. Grease a 12 hole muffin pan. Sift together the flour, baking powder, and salt into a large bowl. Stir in the sugar and apricots.

Mash the bananas and place in a pitcher, then add enough milk to make up the purée to a heaping 1 cup.

Place the eggs in a large pitcher or bowl and beat lightly, then beat in the banana and milk mixture and the oil. Make a well in the center of the dry ingredients and pour in the beaten liquid ingredients. Stir until just combined; do not overmix. Spoon the batter into the muffin pan.

Bake in the preheated oven for 20 minutes, or until well risen, golden brown, and firm to the touch. Let cool in the pan for 5 minutes, then serve warm or transfer to a wire rack to cool completely.

34 Walnut & cinnamon muffins

MAKES 12

2 cups all-purpose flour
1 tbsp baking powder
1 tsp ground cinnamon
pinch of salt
heaping ½ cup light brown sugar
⅔ cup walnuts, coarsely chopped
2 eggs
generous 1 cup milk
6 tbsp sunflower oil or 6 tbsp butter, melted and cooled
1 tsp vanilla extract

Preheat the oven to 400°F/200°C. Line a 12-hole muffin pan with 12 paper liners. Sift together the flour, baking powder, cinnamon, and salt into a large bowl. Stir in the sugar and walnuts.

Place the eggs in a large pitcher or bowl and beat lightly, then beat in the milk, oil, and vanilla extract. Make a well in the center of the dry ingredients and pour in the beaten liquid ingredients. Stir gently until just combined; do not overmix. Spoon the batter into the paper liners.

Bake in the preheated oven for 20 minutes, or until well risen, golden brown, and firm to the touch. Let cool in the pan for 5 minutes, then serve warm or transfer to a wire rack to cool completely.

35 Hazelnut & vanilla seed muffins

Replace the walnuts and cinnamon with ⅔ cup chopped toasted hazelnuts and the seeds from a vanilla bean.

36 Lemon & poppy seed muffins

MAKES 12

2½ cups all-purpose flour
1 tbsp baking powder
heaping ½ cup superfine sugar
2 tbsp poppy seeds
4 tbsp butter
1 large egg, lightly beaten
1 cup milk
finely grated rind and juice of 1 lemon

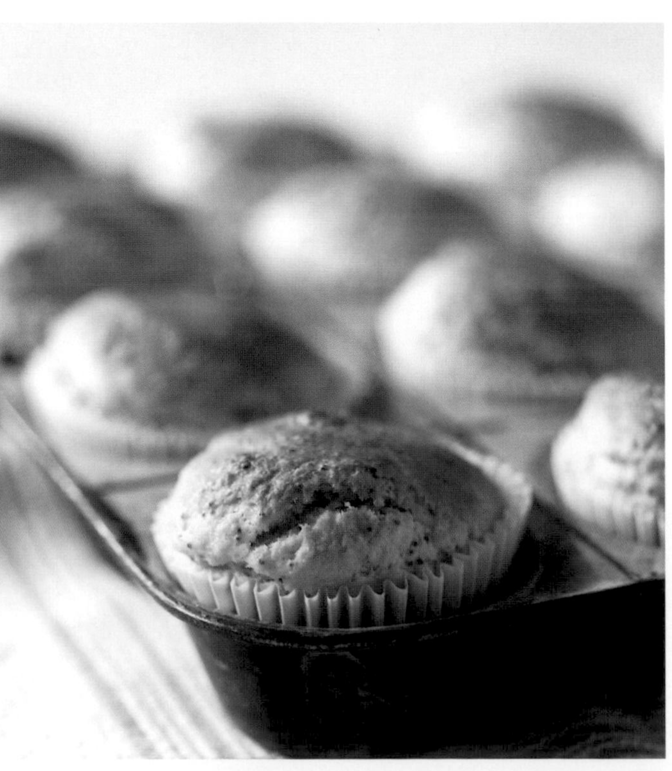

Preheat the oven to 375°F/190°C. Line a 12-hole muffin pan with 12 paper liners. Sift the flour and baking powder into a large bowl and stir in the sugar.

Heat a heavy-bottom skillet over medium–high heat and add the poppy seeds, then toast for about 30 seconds, shaking the skillet to prevent them burning. Remove from the heat and add to the flour mixture.

Place the butter in a saucepan and heat over low heat until melted. Transfer to a bowl and beat with the egg, milk, lemon rind and juice. Pour into the dry mixture and stir well to form a soft, sticky dough. Add a little more milk if it is too dry. Spoon the batter into the paper liners.

Bake in the preheated oven for 25–30 minutes, or until risen, golden brown, and firm to touch. Transfer to a wire rack to cool completely.

37 Cream & spice muffins

MAKES 12

6 tbsp sunflower oil or 6 tbsp butter, melted and cooled, plus extra for greasing
2 cups all-purpose flour
1 tbsp baking powder
1 tsp ground cinnamon
½ tsp ground allspice
½ tsp freshly grated nutmeg
pinch of salt
heaping ½ cup light brown sugar
2 eggs
generous 1 cup heavy cream
confectioners' sugar, for dusting

Preheat the oven to 400°F/200°C. Grease a 12-hole muffin pan. Sift together the flour, baking powder, cinnamon, allspice, nutmeg, and salt into a large bowl. Stir in the brown sugar.

Place the eggs in a large pitcher or bowl and beat lightly, then beat in the cream and oil. Make a well in the center of the dry ingredients and pour in the beaten liquid ingredients. Stir gently until just combined; do not overmix. Spoon the batter into the muffin pan.

Bake in the preheated oven for 20 minutes, or until well risen, golden brown, and firm to the touch. Let cool in the pan for 5 minutes, then serve warm or transfer to a wire rack to cool completely. Dust with sifted confectioners' sugar before serving.

38 With spice butter topping

Blend heaping ⅔ cup butter with 3 tablespoons of confectioners' sugar and 1 teaspoon of pumpkin pie spice, then spread over the cooled muffins.

39 Triple chocolate muffins

MAKES 12

heaping 1¾ cups all-purpose flour
¼ cup unsweetened cocoa
2 tsp baking powder
½ tsp baking soda
½ cup semisweet chocolate chips
½ cup white chocolate chips
scant ½ cup light brown sugar
2 eggs, lightly beaten
1¼ cups sour cream
6 tbsp butter, melted

Preheat the oven to 400°F/200°C. Line a 12-hole muffin pan with 12 paper liners. Sift the flour, cocoa, baking powder, and baking soda into a large bowl, then stir in the semisweet and white chocolate chips. Stir in the sugar.

Place the eggs, sour cream, and butter in a separate bowl and mix well. Add the wet ingredients to the dry ingredients and stir gently until just combined. Spoon the batter into the paper liners.

Bake in the preheated oven for 20 minutes, or until well risen and firm to the touch. Let cool in the pan for 5 minutes, then serve warm or transfer to a wire rack to cool completely.

40 Chocolate & cherry muffins

Replace the white chocolate chips with 3 oz/85 g chopped candied cherries.

41 Oat & cranberry muffins

MAKES 12

6 tbsp sunflower oil, plus extra for greasing
1 cup all-purpose flour
1 tbsp baking powder
heaping ½ cup dark brown sugar
1⅔ cups rolled oats
¾ cup dried cranberries
2 eggs
generous 1 cup buttermilk
1 tsp vanilla extract

Preheat the oven to 400°F/200°C. Grease a 12-hole muffin pan. Sift together the flour and baking powder into a large bowl. Stir in the sugar, oats, and cranberries.

Place the eggs in a large pitcher or bowl and beat lightly, then beat in the buttermilk, oil, and vanilla extract. Make a well in the center of the dry ingredients and pour in the beaten liquid ingredients. Stir gently until just combined; do not overmix. Spoon the batter into the muffin pan.

Bake in the preheated oven for 20 minutes, or until well risen, golden brown, and firm to the touch. Let cool in the pan for 5 minutes, then serve warm or transfer to a wire rack to cool completely.

42 Fresh cranberry oat-topped muffins

Omit the dried cranberries and replace with 1⅓ cups fresh cranberries. Scatter 3 tablespoons of rolled oats over the muffins before baking.

43 Raisin bran muffins

MAKES 12

6 tbsp sunflower oil, plus extra for greasing
1 cup all-purpose flour
1 tbsp baking powder
scant 3 cups wheat bran
heaping ½ cup superfine sugar
1 cup raisins
2 eggs
generous 1 cup skim milk
1 tsp vanilla extract

Preheat the oven to 400°F/200°C. Grease a 12-hole muffin pan. Sift together the flour and baking powder into a large bowl. Stir in the bran, sugar, and raisins.

Place the eggs in a large pitcher or bowl and beat lightly, then beat in the milk, oil, and vanilla extract. Make a well in the center of the dry ingredients and pour in the beaten liquid ingredients. Stir gently until just combined; do not overmix. Spoon the batter into the muffin pan.

Bake in the preheated oven for 20 minutes, or until well risen, golden brown, and firm to the touch. Let cool in the pan for 5 minutes, then serve warm or transfer to a wire rack to cool completely.

44 Healthy oat & prune muffins

MAKES 12

1 cup all-purpose flour
1 tbsp baking powder
heaping ½ cup light brown sugar
1⅓ cups rolled oats
¾ cup pitted prunes, chopped
2 eggs
generous 1 cup buttermilk
6 tbsp sunflower oil
1 tsp vanilla extract

Preheat the oven to 400°F/200°C. Line a 12-hole muffin pan with 12 paper liners. Sift together the flour and baking powder into a large bowl. Stir in the sugar, oats, and prunes.

Place the eggs in a large pitcher or bowl and beat lightly, then beat in the buttermilk, oil, and vanilla extract. Make a well in the center of the dry ingredients and pour in the beaten liquid ingredients. Stir gently until just combined; do not overmix. Spoon the batter into the paper liners.

Bake in the preheated oven for 20 minutes, or until well risen, golden brown, and firm to the touch. Let cool in the pan for 5 minutes, then serve warm or transfer to a wire rack to cool completely.

45 Apricot & sunflower seed muffins

Omit the prunes and replace with ¾ cup chopped soft dried apricots and scatter over 3 tablespoons of sunflower seeds before baking the muffins.

46 Granola muffins

MAKES 12

6 tbsp sunflower oil, plus extra for greasing
¼ cup whole wheat flour
1 cup all-purpose flour
1 tbsp baking powder
scant ½ cup light brown sugar
2 eggs
generous 1 cup skim milk

GRANOLA
scant 1 cup rolled oats
scant ¼ cup blanched almonds, chopped
scant 2 tbsp sunflower seeds
scant ¼ cup raisins
2 tbsp light brown sugar

To make the granola, place the oats in a large, dry skillet and toast over low heat for 1 minute. Add the almonds, sunflower seeds, and raisins and toast for 6–8 minutes, or until browned. Add the sugar and stir for 1 minute until it melts. Remove from the heat and stir until mixed.

Preheat the oven to 400°F/200°C. Grease a 12-hole muffin pan. Sift together both flours and the baking powder into a large bowl, adding any bran left in the strainer. Stir in the sugar and granola.

Place the eggs in a large pitcher or bowl and beat lightly, then beat in the milk and oil. Make a well in the center of the dry ingredients and pour in the beaten liquid ingredients. Stir gently until just combined; do not overmix. Spoon the batter into the muffin pan.

Bake in the preheated oven for 20 minutes, or until well risen, golden brown, and firm to the touch. Let cool in the pan for 5 minutes, then serve warm or transfer to a wire rack to cool completely.

47 Apricot & pecan muffins

Omit the raisins from the granola, add ⅓ cup chopped dried apricots, and replace the almonds with scant ¼ cup chopped pecans.

48 Shredded orange cupcakes

MAKES 12

6 tbsp butter, softened, or soft margarine
½ cup superfine sugar
1 large egg, lightly beaten
⅔ cup self-rising flour
heaping ¼ cup ground almonds
grated rind and juice of 1 small orange

TOPPING
1 orange
¼ cup superfine sugar
1 tbsp toasted slivered almonds

Preheat the oven to 350°F/180°C. Line a 12-hole muffin pan with 12 paper liners. Place the butter and sugar in a large bowl and beat together until light and fluffy, then gradually beat in the egg. Add the flour, ground almonds, and orange rind and fold into the mixture, then fold in the orange juice. Spoon the batter into the paper liners.

Bake in the preheated oven for 20–25 minutes, or until well risen and golden brown.

Meanwhile, make the topping. Using a citrus zester, pare the rind from the orange, then squeeze the juice. Place the rind, juice, and sugar in a saucepan and heat gently, stirring, until the sugar has dissolved, then let simmer for 5 minutes.

When the cupcakes are cooked, prick them all over with a skewer and spoon the warm syrup and rind over each cake.

Scatter the slivered almonds on top and transfer to a wire rack to cool completely.

49 Shredded lemon cupcakes

Replace the orange rind and juice with lemon rind and juice.

50 Lime & coconut cupcakes

Replace the orange rind and juice in the cake with the rind and juice of 1½ limes. Add ¼ cup dry unsweetened coconut to the batter. For the topping, use the pared rind of 1 lime and the juice of 2 limes in place of the orange. Replace the almonds with toasted dry unsweetened coconut.

51 Mocha cupcakes with whipped cream

MAKES 20

2 tbsp instant espresso coffee powder
6 tbsp butter
½ cup superfine sugar
1 tbsp honey
generous ¾ cup water
1⅔ cups all-purpose flour
2 tbsp unsweetened cocoa
1 tsp baking soda
3 tbsp milk
1 large egg, lightly beaten

TOPPING
1 cup whipping cream
unsweetened cocoa, for dusting

Preheat the oven to 350°F/180°C. Line two 12-hole muffin pans with 20 paper liners. Place the coffee powder, butter, sugar, honey, and water in a saucepan and heat gently, stirring, until the sugar has dissolved. Bring to a boil, then reduce the heat and let simmer for 5 minutes. Pour into a large heatproof bowl and let cool. When the mixture has cooled, sift in the flour and cocoa. Place the baking soda and milk in a bowl and stir to dissolve, then add to the mixture with the egg and beat together until smooth. Spoon the batter into the paper liners.

Bake in the preheated oven for 15–20 minutes, or until well risen and firm to the touch. Transfer to a wire rack to cool completely.

For the topping, place the cream in a bowl and whip until it holds its shape. Spoon heaping teaspoonfuls of cream on top of each cake, then dust lightly with sifted cocoa.

52 Mocha walnut cupcakes

Add ¼ cup chopped walnuts to the batter. For the topping, dissolve 2 teaspoons of coffee powder in 1 tablespoon of boiling water and let cool. Lightly whip the cream until it begins to hold its shape, then add the coffee and 2 tablespoons of confectioners' sugar and whip until soft peaks form. Spread on the cakes and decorate with walnut halves.

53 Peaches 'n' cream cupcakes

Makes 12

14 oz/400 g canned peach slices in fruit juice
8 tbsp butter, softened
heaping ½ cup superfine sugar
2 eggs, lightly beaten
heaping ¾ cup self-rising flour
¾ cup heavy cream

Preheat the oven to 350°F/180°C. Line a 12-hole muffin pan with 12 paper liners. Drain the peaches, reserving the juice. Set aside 12 small slices and finely chop the remaining slices.

Place the butter and sugar in a large bowl and beat together until light and fluffy. Gradually beat in the eggs. Sift in the flour and fold into the mixture. Fold in the chopped peaches and 1 tablespoon of the reserved juice. Spoon the batter into the paper liners.

Bake in the oven for 25 minutes, or until golden brown. Let the cupcakes cool in the pan for 10 minutes, then transfer to a wire rack to cool completely.

When ready to decorate, place the cream in a bowl and whip until soft peaks form. Spread the cream on top of the cupcakes, using a knife to form the cream into peaks. Place the reserved peach slices on top to decorate.

54 Apricot cream cupcakes

Use 8 apricot halves in fruit juice instead of the peach slices. Slice 4 halves into 3 slices each and set aside for decoration. Finely chop the 4 remaining apricot halves and add to the batter with 1 tablespoon of juice from the can.

55 Dried apricot cupcakes

Replace the can of peach slices with ½ cup finely chopped plumped dried apricots and add 1 tablespoon of orange juice to replace the fruit juice from the can. To decorate, dust lightly with sifted confectioners' sugar.

56 *Moist walnut cupcakes*

MAKES 12

heaping ¾ cup walnuts
4 tbsp butter, softened, cut into small pieces
½ cup superfine sugar
grated rind of ½ lemon
½ cup self-rising flour
2 eggs
12 walnut halves, for decorating

FROSTING
4 tbsp butter, softened
¾ cup confectioners' sugar
grated rind of ½ lemon
1 tsp lemon juice

Preheat the oven to 375°F/190°C. Line a 12-hole muffin pan with 12 paper liners. Place the walnuts in a food processor and pulse until finely ground. Be careful not to overgrind, or the nuts will turn to oil.

Add the butter, sugar, lemon rind, flour, and eggs and blend until the mixture is evenly combined. Spoon the batter into the paper liners.

Bake in the preheated oven for 20 minutes, or until well risen and golden brown. Transfer to a wire rack to cool completely.

To make the frosting, place the butter in a bowl and beat until fluffy. Sift in the confectioners' sugar, add the lemon rind and juice, and mix well together. When the cupcakes are cold, spread the frosting on top of each cupcake and top with a walnut to decorate.

57 *Sticky orange & walnut cupcakes*

For the cupcakes, replace the lemon rind with orange rind. Instead of the frosting, heat 6 tablespoons of orange juice with 2 tablespoons of superfine sugar, stirring until the sugar dissolves, then boil until syrupy. Spoon the syrup over the hot cakes and let cool before serving.

58 *Moist pecan cupcakes*

Replace the walnuts with pecans and the lemon rind and juice with orange rind and juice.

59 *Feathered-iced coffee cupcakes*

MAKES 16

1 tbsp instant coffee granules
1 tbsp boiling water
8 tbsp butter, softened, or soft margarine
½ cup light brown sugar
2 eggs
heaping ¾ cup self-rising flour
½ tsp baking powder
2 tbsp sour cream

ICING
2 cups confectioners' sugar
4 tsp warm water
1 tsp instant coffee granules
2 tsp boiling water

Preheat the oven to 375°F/190°C. Line two 12-hole muffin pans with 16 paper liners. Place the coffee granules in a cup or small bowl, add the boiling water, and stir until dissolved. Let cool slightly. Place the butter, sugar, and eggs in a large bowl. Sift in the flour and baking powder and beat until smooth. Add the dissolved coffee and sour cream and beat until mixed. Spoon the batter into the paper liners.

Bake in the preheated oven for 20 minutes, or until well risen and golden. Cool on a wire rack.

To make the icing, sift ¾ cup of the confectioners' sugar into a bowl and add enough warm water to mix until thick enough to coat the back of a wooden spoon. Dissolve the coffee in the boiling water. Sift the remaining confectioners' sugar into a bowl and stir in the dissolved coffee. Ice the cakes with the white icing, then pipe the coffee icing in parallel lines on top. Draw a skewer across the piped lines in both directions. Let set.

60 *Feathered-iced mocha cupcakes*

Replace the sour cream with 2 oz/55 g melted semisweet chocolate.

61 *Feathered-iced chocolate cupcakes*

Replace the coffee granules for the cake batter with unsweetened cocoa. To complete the cakes, melt 6 oz/175 g milk chocolate and 1 oz/25 g white chocolate in separate bowls and spoon the white chocolate into a pastry bag fitted with a piping tip. Spread the milk chocolate over the top of the cakes, then quickly pipe the white chocolate in lines across the cakes. Drag a skewer across the piped lines in both directions to feather the chocolate.

62 Queen cakes

MAKES 18

8 tbsp butter, softened, or soft margarine
½ cup superfine sugar
2 large eggs, lightly beaten
4 tsp lemon juice
1¼ cups self-rising flour
¾ cup raisins
2–4 tbsp milk, if necessary

Preheat the oven to 375°F/190°C. Line two 12-hole muffin pans with 18 paper liners. Place the butter and sugar in a large bowl and beat together until light and fluffy. Gradually beat in the eggs, then beat in the lemon juice with 1 tablespoon of the flour. Fold in the remaining flour and the raisins. If necessary, add a little milk to create a soft dropping consistency. Spoon the batter into the paper liners.

Bake in the preheated oven for 15–20 minutes, or until well risen and golden brown. Transfer to a wire rack to cool completely.

63 Orange queen cakes

Replace the lemon juice with orange juice and add the grated rind of ½ orange with the juice.

64 Iced queen cakes

Sift 1⅓ cups confectioners' sugar into a small bowl and stir in about 4 teaspoons of lemon juice. Mix to a smooth icing that coats the back of a wooden spoon. Spread the icing over the cakes almost to the edges.

65 Carrot & orange cupcakes

MAKES 12

8 tbsp butter, softened, or soft margarine
heaping ½ cup light brown sugar
juice and finely grated rind of 1 small orange
2 large eggs, lightly beaten
heaping 1 cup grated carrot
¼ cup walnut pieces, coarsely chopped
1 cup all-purpose flour
1 tsp ground pumpkin pie spice
1½ tsp baking powder

FROSTING
1¼ cups mascarpone cheese
4 tbsp confectioners' sugar
grated rind of 1 large orange

Preheat the oven to 350°F/180°C. Line a 12-hole muffin pan with 12 paper liners.

Place the butter, sugar, and orange rind in a bowl and beat together until light and fluffy, then gradually beat in the eggs. Squeeze any excess liquid from the carrots and add to the mixture with the walnuts and orange juice. Stir until well mixed. Sift in the flour, pumpkin pie spice, and baking powder and fold in. Spoon the batter into the paper liners.

Bake in the preheated oven for 25 minutes, or until risen, firm to the touch, and golden brown. Transfer to a wire rack to cool completely.

To make the frosting, place the mascarpone cheese, confectioners' sugar, and orange rind in a large bowl and beat together until they are well mixed.

When the cupcakes are cold, spread the frosting on top of each cupcake, swirling it with a round-bladed knife.

66 Carrot & lemon cupcakes

Replace the orange rind and juice in the cakes with lemon rind and juice. Instead of the frosting, sift 1½ cups confectioners' sugar into a large bowl and beat in enough lemon juice to make a smooth icing. Spread on top of the cakes and leave plain or decorate with lemon candy slices.

67 Chocolate carrot cupcakes

Add 3 oz/85 g semisweet chocolate chips along with the carrot. Beat 2 oz/55 g melted semisweet chocolate into the mascarpone frosting before spreading on the cupcakes.

68 Chocolate cupcakes with cream cheese frosting

MAKES 18

6 tbsp butter, softened, or soft margarine
½ cup superfine sugar
2 eggs, lightly beaten
2 tbsp milk
⅓ cup semisweet chocolate chips
1⅔ cups self-rising flour
¼ cup unsweetened cocoa

TOPPING
8 oz/225 g white chocolate, broken into pieces
⅔ cup low-fat cream cheese
chocolate curls, for decorating

Preheat the oven to 400°F/200°C. Line two 12-hole muffin pans with 18 paper liners.

Place the butter and sugar in a large bowl and beat together until light and fluffy, then gradually beat in the eggs. Add the milk, then fold in the chocolate chips. Sift in the flour and cocoa, then fold into the batter. Spoon the batter into the paper liners and smooth the tops.

Bake in the preheated oven for 20 minutes, or until well risen and springy to the touch. Transfer to a wire rack to cool completely.

To make the frosting, place the chocolate in a small heatproof bowl, set the bowl over a saucepan of gently simmering water, and heat until melted. Let cool slightly. Place the cream cheese in a separate bowl and beat until softened, then beat in the slightly cooled chocolate.

When the cupcakes are cold, spread a little of the frosting over the top of each cupcake, then let chill in the refrigerator for 1 hour before serving. Decorate with a few chocolate curls, if liked.

69 White chocolate cupcakes

Replace the semisweet chocolate chips with ½ cup white chocolate chips. Omit the cocoa and increase the flour to 1¾ cups. Decorate with white chocolate curls made with a vegetable peeler.

70 With chocolate mascarpone frosting

For the frosting, replace the cream cheese with mascarpone and decorate with milk chocolate curls.

71 Lemon butterfly cakes

MAKES 12

heaping ¾ cup self-rising flour
½ tsp baking powder
8 tbsp butter, softened
heaping ½ cup superfine sugar
2 eggs
finely grated rind of ½ lemon
2 tbsp milk
confectioners' sugar, for dusting

LEMON BUTTERCREAM
6 tbsp butter, softened
1½ cups confectioners' sugar
1 tbsp lemon juice

Preheat the oven to 375°F/190°C. Line a 12-hole muffin pan with 12 paper liners.

Sift the flour and baking powder into a large bowl, add the butter, sugar, eggs, lemon rind, and milk, and beat together until smooth. Spoon the batter into the paper liners.

Bake in the preheated oven for 15–20 minutes, or until well risen and golden brown. Transfer to a wire rack to cool completely.

To make the frosting, place the butter in a bowl and beat until fluffy. Sift in the confectioners' sugar, add the lemon juice, and beat together until smooth and creamy. When the cupcakes are cold, cut the top off each cake then cut the top in half.

Spread or pipe a little of the lemon frosting over the cut surface of each cupcake, then gently press the 2 cut cake pieces into it at an angle to resemble butterfly wings. Dust with sifted confectioners' sugar before serving.

72 Orange butterfly cakes

Replace the lemon rind and juice with orange rind and juice.

73 Vanilla butterfly cakes

Omit the lemon rind from the cake batter and replace the lemon juice in the frosting with 1 teaspoon of vanilla extract. Decorate with sugar sprinkles, if liked.

74 Apple streusel cupcakes

MAKES 14

½ tsp baking soda
10 oz/280 g jar applesauce
4 tbsp butter, softened,
or soft margarine
½ cup raw brown sugar
1 large egg, lightly beaten
1¼ cups self-rising flour
½ tsp ground cinnamon
½ tsp freshly ground nutmeg

TOPPING
⅓ cup all-purpose flour
¼ cup raw brown sugar
¼ tsp ground cinnamon
¼ tsp freshly grated nutmeg
3 heaping tbsp butter,
cut into small pieces

Preheat the oven to 350°F/180°C. Line two 12-hole muffin pans with 14 paper liners.

First, make the topping. Place the flour, sugar, cinnamon, and nutmeg in a large bowl. Add the butter and rub it in with your fingertips until the mixture resembles fine breadcrumbs. Set aside until required.

To make the cupcakes, add the baking soda to the jar of applesauce and stir until dissolved. Place the butter and sugar in a large bowl and beat together until light and fluffy, then gradually beat in the egg. Sift in the flour, cinnamon, and nutmeg and fold into the batter, alternating with the applesauce. Spoon the batter into the paper liners. Scatter the reserved topping over each cupcake to cover the tops and press down gently. Bake in the preheated oven for 20 minutes, or until well risen and golden brown. Leave the cakes for 2–3 minutes in the pans before serving warm, or transfer to a wire rack to cool completely.

75 Apricot streusel cupcakes

Drain 10 oz/280 g canned apricots, reserving the juice. Chop the apricots and mix a little of the juice with 1 teaspoon of cornstarch. Place the apricots in a saucepan with the juice and bring to a boil. Add the cornstarch mixture, and cook over low heat, stirring, until thickened. Let cool, then complete as before, replacing the applesauce with the apricot mixture.

76 Cranberry streusel cupcakes

Replace the applesauce with cranberry sauce.

77 Cherry streusel cupcakes

Replace the applesauce with 7 oz/200 g canned cherry pie filling.

78 Raspberry crumble muffins

MAKES 12

6 tbsp sunflower oil or 6 tbsp butter, melted and cooled, plus extra for greasing
2 cups all-purpose flour
1 tbsp baking powder
½ tsp baking soda
pinch of salt
heaping ½ cup superfine sugar
2 eggs
heaping 1 cup plain yogurt
1 tsp vanilla extract
1 cup frozen raspberries

CRUMBLE TOPPING
⅓ cup all-purpose flour
2½ tbsp butter, cut into pieces
2 tbsp superfine sugar

Preheat the oven to 400°F/200°C. Grease a 12-hole muffin pan.

To make the crumble topping, place the flour into a bowl. Add the butter and rub it in with your fingertips until the mixture resembles fine breadcrumbs. Stir in the sugar and set aside.

To make the muffins, sift together the flour, baking powder, baking soda, and salt into a large bowl. Stir in the sugar. Place the eggs in a large pitcher or bowl and beat lightly, then beat in the yogurt, oil, and vanilla extract. Make a well in the center of the dry ingredients, pour in the beaten liquid ingredients, and add the raspberries.

Stir gently until just combined; do not overmix. Spoon the batter into the muffin pan. Scatter the crumble topping over each muffin and then press down lightly.

Bake in the preheated oven for 20 minutes, or until well risen, golden brown, and firm to the touch. Let cool in the pan for 5 minutes, then serve warm or transfer to a wire rack to cool completely.

79 With almond crunch topping

Add ⅓ cup chopped toasted slivered almonds and 6 crushed amaretti cookies to the crumble topping before scattering over the muffins.

80 Sour cream & pineapple muffins

MAKES 12

6 tbsp sunflower oil or 6 tbsp butter, melted and cooled, plus extra for greasing
2 slices canned pineapple slices in natural juice, plus 2 tbsp juice from the can
2 cups all-purpose flour
1 tbsp baking powder
pinch of salt
heaping ½ cup superfine sugar
2 eggs
heaping ¾ cup sour cream
1 tsp vanilla extract

Preheat the oven to 400°F/200°C. Grease a 12-hole muffin pan. Drain and finely chop the pineapple slices.

Sift together the flour, baking powder, and salt into a large bowl. Stir in the sugar and chopped pineapple.

Place the eggs in a large pitcher or bowl and beat lightly, then beat in the sour cream, oil, pineapple juice, and vanilla extract. Make a well in the center of the dry ingredients and pour in the beaten liquid ingredients. Stir gently until just combined; do not overmix. Spoon the batter into the muffin pan.

Bake in the preheated oven for 20 minutes, or until well risen, golden brown, and firm to the touch. Let cool in the pan for 5 minutes, then serve warm or transfer to a wire rack to cool completely.

81 With pineapple frosting

Beat scant ½ cup cream cheese with 2 tablespoons of confectioners' sugar and 1 tablespoon of pineapple juice, then spread over the cooled muffins.

82 Spicy apple & oat muffins

Makes 12

6 tbsp sunflower oil, plus extra for greasing
1 cup all-purpose flour
1 tbsp baking powder
1 tsp apple pie spice
heaping ⅓ cup light brown sugar
2 cups rolled oats
1 large apple
2 eggs
½ cup skim milk
½ cup fresh apple juice

Preheat the oven to 400°F/200°C. Grease a 12-hole muffin pan. Sift together the flour, baking powder, and apple pie spice into a large bowl. Stir in the sugar and 1⅔ cups of the oats.

Finely chop the unpeeled apple, discarding the core. Add to the flour mixture and stir together.

Place the eggs in a large pitcher or bowl and beat lightly, then beat in the milk, apple juice, and oil. Make a well in the center of the dry ingredients and pour in the beaten liquid ingredients. Stir gently until just combined; do not overmix. Spoon the batter into the muffin pan and sprinkle the tops with the remaining oats.

Bake in the preheated oven for 20 minutes, or until well risen, golden brown, and firm to the touch. Let cool in the pan for 5 minutes, then serve warm or transfer to a wire rack to cool completely.

83 Pear, oat & nutmeg muffins

Replace the apple and apple juice with 2 medium peeled, cored, and chopped pears and pear juice, and add ½ teaspoon of ground nutmeg.

84 Spicy dried fruit muffins

Makes 12

6 tbsp sunflower oil or 6 tbsp butter, melted and cooled
2 cups all-purpose flour
1 tbsp baking powder
1 tbsp apple pie spice
pinch of salt
heaping ½ cup superfine sugar
heaping 1 cup mixed dried fruit
2 eggs
generous 1 cup milk

Preheat the oven to 400°F/200°C. Line a 12-hole muffin pan with 12 paper liners. Sift together the flour, baking powder, apple pie spice, and salt into a large bowl. Stir in the sugar and dried fruit.

Place the eggs in a large pitcher or bowl and beat lightly, then beat in the milk and oil. Make a well in the center of the dry ingredients and pour in the beaten liquid ingredients. Stir gently until just combined; do not overmix. Spoon the batter into the paper liners.

Bake in the preheated oven for 20 minutes, or until well risen, golden brown, and firm to the touch. Let cool in the pan for 5 minutes, then serve warm or transfer to a wire rack to cool completely.

85 With brandy cream

Whip heaping ¾ cup heavy cream with 1 tablespoon of brandy and 1 tablespoon of superfine sugar until stiff, then spoon onto the cooled muffins.

86 Apple & cinnamon muffins

MAKES 12

scant 1½ cups whole wheat flour
½ cup fine oats
2 tsp baking powder
scant ⅔ cup light brown sugar
2 large eggs
1 cup low-fat milk
generous ⅓ cup peanut oil
1 tsp vanilla extract
1 tsp ground cinnamon
1 large baking apple

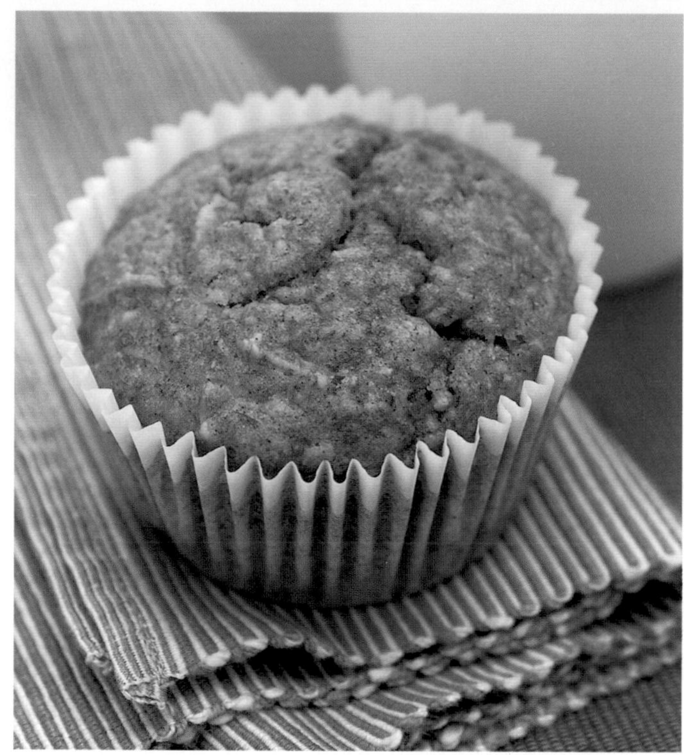

Preheat the oven to 350°F/180°C. Line a 12-hole muffin pan with paper liners.

Sift the flour, oats, and baking powder together into a large bowl, then add the larger particles left in the strainer. Stir in the sugar. Place the eggs, milk, and oil in a separate bowl and beat together until well combined. Add to the dry ingredients, along with the vanilla extract and cinnamon, and stir until just combined; do not overmix.

Peel, core, and grate the apple and stir into the batter, then spoon the batter into the paper liners.

Bake in the preheated oven for 20–25 minutes, or until risen and golden brown. Let cool in the pan for a few minutes before serving warm or transfer to a wire rack to cool completely.

87 Buttermilk berry muffins

MAKES 12

6 tbsp sunflower oil or 6 tbsp butter, melted and cooled, plus extra for greasing
heaping 1 cup frozen mixed berries, such as blueberries, raspberries, blackberries, strawberries
2 cups all-purpose flour
1 tbsp baking powder
pinch of salt
heaping ½ cup superfine sugar
2 eggs
generous 1 cup buttermilk
1 tsp vanilla extract
confectioners' sugar, for dusting

Preheat the oven to 400°F/200°C. Grease a 12-hole muffin pan. Cut any large berries, such as strawberries, into small pieces.

Sift together the flour, baking powder, and salt into a large bowl. Stir in the sugar.

Place the eggs in a large pitcher or bowl and beat lightly, then beat in the buttermilk, oil, and vanilla extract. Make a well in the center of the dry ingredients, pour in the beaten liquid ingredients, and add the berries. Stir until combined; do not overmix. Spoon the batter into the muffin pan.

Bake in the preheated oven for 20 minutes, or until well risen, golden brown, and firm to the touch. Let cool in the pan for 5 minutes, then serve warm or transfer to a wire rack to cool completely. Dust with a little sifted confectioners' sugar before serving.

88 Buttermilk cranberry muffins

Replace the frozen berries with 1½ cups frozen cranberries mixed with ½ teaspoon of finely grated orange rind.

89 Frosted chocolate orange muffins

MAKES 12

6 tbsp sunflower oil or 6 tbsp butter, melted and cooled, plus extra for greasing
2 oranges
about ½ cup milk
1⅔ cups all-purpose flour
½ cup unsweetened cocoa
1 tbsp baking powder
pinch of salt
heaping ½ cup light brown sugar
scant 1 cup semisweet chocolate chips
2 eggs
strips of orange zest, for decorating

FROSTING
2 oz/55 g semisweet chocolate, broken into pieces
2 tbsp butter
2 tbsp water
1½ cups confectioners' sugar

Preheat the oven to 400°F/200°C. Grease a 12-hole muffin pan. Finely grate the rind from the oranges and squeeze the juice. Add enough milk to make up the juice to a heaping 1 cup, then add the orange rind. Sift together the flour, cocoa, baking powder, and salt into a large bowl. Stir in the brown sugar and chocolate chips.

Place the eggs in a large pitcher or bowl and beat lightly, then beat in the milk and orange mixture and the oil. Make a well in the center of the dry ingredients and pour in the beaten liquid ingredients. Stir gently until just combined; do not overmix. Spoon the batter into the muffin pan.

Bake in the preheated oven for 20 minutes, or until well risen and firm to the touch. Let cool in the pan for 5 minutes, then transfer to a wire rack to cool completely.

To make the frosting, place the chocolate in a heatproof bowl, add the butter and water, then set the bowl over a saucepan of gently simmering water and heat, stirring, until melted. Remove from the heat, sift in the confectioners' sugar, and beat until smooth, then spread the frosting on top of the muffins and decorate with strips of orange zest.

90 With white chocolate frosting

Replace the semisweet chocolate with 2 oz/55 g white chocolate and top the muffins with crushed orange flavored chocolate.

91 Brandied peach muffins

MAKES 12

14 oz/400 g canned peaches in natural juice
2 cups all-purpose flour
1 tbsp baking powder
pinch of salt
heaping ½ cup superfine sugar
2 eggs
¾ cup buttermilk
6 tbsp sunflower oil or 6 tbsp butter, melted and cooled
3 tbsp brandy
finely grated rind of 1 orange

Preheat the oven to 400°F/200°C. Line a 12-hole muffin pan with 12 paper liners. Drain and finely chop the peaches. Sift together the flour, baking powder, and salt into a large bowl. Stir in the sugar.

Place the eggs in a large pitcher or bowl and beat lightly, then beat in the buttermilk, oil, brandy, and orange rind. Make a well in the center of the dry ingredients, pour in the beaten liquid ingredients, and add the chopped peaches. Stir gently until just combined; do not overmix. Spoon the batter into the paper liners.

Bake in the preheated oven for 20 minutes, or until well risen, golden brown, and firm to the touch. Let cool in the pan for 5 minutes, then serve warm or transfer to a wire rack to cool completely.

92 Pear and liqueur muffins

Replace the peaches with 14 oz/400 g canned pears, drained and chopped, and use Poire William liqueur to replace the brandy.

93 *Warm molten-centered chocolate cupcakes*

Makes 8

4 tbsp butter, softened, or soft margarine
¼ cup superfine sugar
1 large egg
⅔ cup self-rising flour
1 tbsp unsweetened cocoa
2 oz/55 g semisweet chocolate
confectioners' sugar, for dusting

Preheat the oven to 375°F/190°C. Line a 12-hole muffin pan with 8 paper liners.

Place the butter, sugar, egg, flour, and cocoa in a large bowl and beat together until just smooth. Spoon half of the batter into the paper liners. Using a teaspoon, make an indentation in the center of each cake. Break the chocolate into 8 even squares and place a piece in each indentation, then spoon the remaining cake batter on top.

Bake in the preheated oven for 20 minutes, or until well risen and springy to the touch. Leave the cupcakes in the pan for 2–3 minutes before serving warm, dusted with sifted confectioners' sugar.

94 *White chocolate-centered cupcakes*

Replace the semisweet chocolate with squares of white chocolate.

95 *Vanilla & chocolate cupcakes*

Increase the flour to ¾ cup and omit the cocoa. Add ½ teaspoon of vanilla extract to the butter and sugar, and use milk chocolate instead of the semisweet chocolate.

96 *Chocolate cherry cupcakes*

Makes 12

1¾ oz/50 g semisweet chocolate, broken into pieces
4½ tbsp butter
⅓ cup cherry jam
⅓ cup superfine sugar
2 large eggs
¾ cup self-rising flour

TOPPING
4 tsp Kirsch liqueur
⅔ cup heavy cream
12 fresh, candied, or maraschino cherries
chocolate curls, for decorating

Preheat the oven to 350°F/180°C. Line a 12-hole muffin pan with 12 paper liners. Place the chocolate and butter in a saucepan and heat gently, stirring continuously, until melted. Pour into a large bowl, then stir until smooth and let cool slightly. Add the jam, sugar, and eggs to the cooled chocolate and beat together. Add the flour and stir together until combined. Spoon the batter into the paper liners.

Bake in the preheated oven for 20 minutes, or until firm to the touch. Let cool in the pan for 10 minutes, then transfer to a wire rack to cool completely.

When the cupcakes are cold, sprinkle the Kirsch over the tops of each and let soak for at least 15 minutes.

When ready to decorate, place the cream in a bowl and whip until soft peaks form. Spread the cream on top of the cupcakes with a knife to form the cream into peaks. Top each cupcake with a cherry and decorate with chocolate curls.

97 *Chocolate strawberry cupcakes*

Replace the cherry jam with strawberry jam and sprinkle the cold cupcakes with brandy instead of Kirsch. Decorate each cupcake with a small whole strawberry.

98 *Warm strawberry cupcakes baked in a teacup*

MAKES 6

8 tbsp butter, softened, plus extra for greasing
4 tbsp strawberry preserve
heaping ½ cup superfine sugar
2 eggs, lightly beaten
1 tsp vanilla extract
heaping ¾ cup self-rising flour
6 whole strawberries, for decorating
confectioners' sugar, for dusting

Preheat the oven to 350°F/180°C. Grease six ¾-cup capacity heavy round teacups with butter. Spoon 2 teaspoons of the strawberry preserve into the bottom of each teacup.

Place the butter and sugar in a large bowl and beat together until light and fluffy. Gradually add the eggs, beating well after each addition, then add the vanilla extract. Sift in the flour and fold into the batter. Spoon the batter into the teacups.

Stand the cups in a roasting pan, then pour in enough hot water to come one third up the sides of the cups. Bake in the preheated oven for 40 minutes, or until well risen and golden brown, and a skewer, inserted in the center, comes out clean. If overbrowning, cover the cupcakes with a sheet of foil. Let the cupcakes cool for 2–3 minutes, then carefully lift the cups from the pan and place them on saucers.

Top each cupcake with a strawberry, then dust them with sifted confectioners' sugar. Serve warm with the remaining strawberries on the side.

99 *Warm raspberry cupcakes*

Replace the strawberry preserve with raspberry preserve and decorate with fresh raspberries.

100 *Warm peach cupcakes*

Replace the strawberry preserve with a few well-drained, canned peach slices and decorate with extra peach slices.

101 *Tropical pineapple cupcakes*

MAKES 12

2 slices canned pineapple in natural juice
6 tbsp butter, softened, or soft margarine
½ cup superfine sugar
1 large egg, lightly beaten
⅔ cup self-rising flour

FROSTING
2 tbsp butter, softened
½ cup soft cream cheese
grated rind of 1 lemon or lime
heaping ¾ cup confectioners' sugar
1 tsp lemon juice or lime juice

Preheat the oven to 350°F/180°C. Line a 12-hole muffin pan with 12 paper liners. Drain the pineapple, reserving the juice.

Finely chop the pineapple slices. Place the butter and sugar in a large bowl and beat together until light and fluffy, then gradually beat in the egg. Add the flour and fold into the mixture. Fold in the chopped pineapple and 1 tablespoon of the reserved pineapple juice. Spoon the batter into the paper liners. Bake in the preheated oven for 20 minutes, or until well risen and golden brown. Transfer to a wire rack to cool completely.

To make the frosting, place the butter and cream cheese in a large bowl and beat together until smooth, then add the lemon or lime rind.

Sift the confectioners' sugar into the mixture and beat together until well mixed. Gradually beat in the lemon or lime juice, adding enough to form a spreading consistency.

When the cupcakes are cold, spread the frosting on top of each cake, or fill a pastry bag fitted with a large star tip and pipe the frosting on top.

102 *Pina colada cupcakes*

Add ¼ cup dry unsweetened coconut and an extra ½ tablespoon of pineapple juice to the cake batter. For the frosting, beat 2 tablespoons of dry unsweetened coconut into the frosting and replace the lemon or lime juice with rum.

103 *Naughty but nice cupcakes*

MAKES 9

2½ oz/70 g semisweet chocolate, broken into pieces, plus extra for decorating
heaping ¾ cup butter
¾ cup superfine sugar
2 large eggs, lightly beaten
2 tbsp brandy
1¼ cups self-rising flour

TOPPING
heaping ¾ cup heavy cream
1 tbsp confectioners' sugar
1 tbsp brandy
9 large ripe strawberries

Preheat the oven to 350°F/180°C. Line a 12-hole muffin pan with 9 paper liners. Place the chocolate in a heatproof bowl, set the bowl over a saucepan of gently simmering water, and heat until melted. Remove from the heat and let cool. Place the butter and sugar in a large bowl and beat together until light and fluffy, then gradually beat in the eggs. Stir in the brandy, followed by the melted chocolate, then carefully fold in the flour. Spoon the batter into the paper liners.

Bake in the preheated oven for 20–25 minutes, or until golden and springy to the touch. Transfer to a wire rack to cool completely.

To decorate, place the cream, sugar, and brandy in a bowl and whip together until just stiff. Spoon the cream into a pastry bag fitted with a star tip and pipe a generous swirl of cream on top of each cake, then place a strawberry on top.

104 *Nice & naughty cupcakes*

Add 1 cup raspberries to the cake batter and decorate with extra raspberries instead of the strawberries.

105 *Warm spiced apple pie cupcakes*

MAKES 12

3½ tbsp butter, softened
⅓ cup raw brown sugar
1 egg, lightly beaten
heaping 1 cup all-purpose flour
1½ tsp baking powder
½ tsp apple pie spice
1 large baking apple, peeled, cored, and finely chopped
1 tbsp orange juice

TOPPING
5 tbsp all-purpose flour
½ tsp apple pie spice
2 tbsp butter
¼ cup superfine sugar

Preheat the oven to 350°F/180°C. Line a 12-hole muffin pan with 12 paper liners.

To make the topping, place the flour, apple pie spice, butter, and sugar in a large bowl and rub in with your fingertips until the mixture resembles fine breadcrumbs. Set aside.

To make the cupcakes, place the butter and sugar in a large bowl and beat together until light and fluffy, then gradually beat in the egg. Sift in the flour, baking powder, and apple pie spice and fold into the mixture, then fold in the chopped apple and orange juice. Spoon the batter into the paper liners. Add the topping to cover the top of each cupcake and press down gently.

Bake in the preheated oven for 30 minutes, or until golden brown. Let the cupcakes cool in the pan for 2–3 minutes and serve warm, or let cool for 10 minutes and then transfer to a wire rack to cool completely.

106 *Chocolate zucchini cupcakes*

MAKES 12

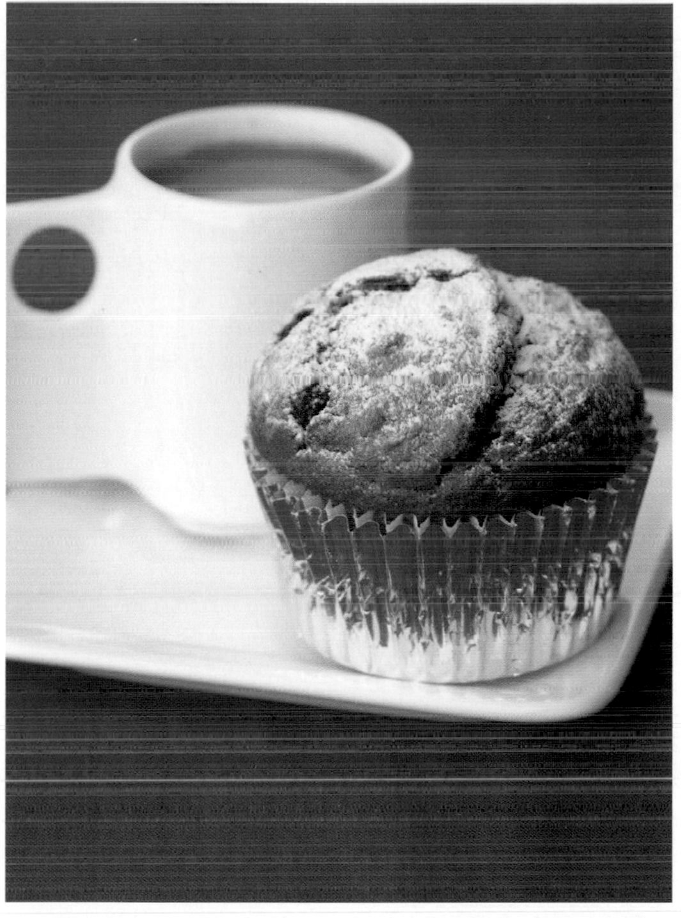

1 small zucchini
3 oz/85 g semisweet chocolate, broken into pieces
2 large eggs
¼ cup light brown sugar
⅓ cup sunflower oil
heaping ¾ cup all-purpose flour
½ tsp baking powder
¼ tsp baking soda
1 tbsp pecans, finely chopped
confectioners' sugar, for dusting

Preheat the oven to 350°F/180°C. Line a 12-hole muffin pan with 12 paper liners. Peel and grate the zucchini, discarding any liquid. Set aside.

Place the chocolate in a heatproof bowl, set the bowl over a saucepan of gently simmering water, and heat until melted. Remove from the heat and stir until smooth. Let cool slightly.

Place the eggs, sugar, and oil in a large bowl and whisk together. Sift in the flour, baking powder, and baking soda and stir together until mixed. Stir in the zucchini, pecans, and melted chocolate until combined. Spoon the batter into the paper liners.

Bake in the preheated oven for 25 minutes, or until firm to the touch. Let the cupcakes cool in the pan for 10 minutes, then transfer to a wire rack to cool completely. When the cupcakes are cold, dust with sifted confectioners' sugar.

107 *Marbled chocolate cupcakes*

MAKES 21

¾ cup soft margarine
1 cup superfine sugar
3 eggs
1¼ cups self-rising flour
2 tbsp milk
2 oz/55 g semisweet chocolate, melted

Preheat the oven to 350°F/180°C. Line two 12-hole muffin pans with 21 paper liners. Place the margarine, sugar, eggs, flour, and milk in a large bowl and beat together until just smooth. Divide the batter among 2 bowls. Add the melted chocolate to one and stir until mixed. Using a teaspoon, and alternating the chocolate batter with the plain, put 4 half-teaspoons into each case.

Bake in the preheated oven for 20 minutes, or until well risen. Transfer to a wire rack to cool.

108 *Chocolate orange marbled cupcakes*

Add the grated rind and juice of ½ small orange and a few drops of orange food coloring to the plain cake batter.

109 *Iced marbled cupcakes*

Make the cakes as usual. Sift 2¼ cups confectioners' sugar into a bowl and stir in 2–3 tablespoons of water until smooth. Divide the icing in half and add 1 tablespoon of cocoa to one portion, adding a little extra water if required. Spoon small amounts of each icing on top of the cakes and marble together to cover the cakes with the tip of a knife.

110 *Maple pecan muffins*

Makes 12

2 cups all-purpose flour
1 tbsp baking powder
pinch of salt
heaping ½ cup superfine sugar
⅔ cup pecans, coarsely chopped
2 eggs
¾ cup buttermilk
generous ¼ cup maple syrup, plus extra for glazing
6 tbsp sunflower oil or 6 tbsp butter, melted and cooled
12 pecan halves

Preheat the oven to 400°F/200°C. Line a 12-hole muffin pan with 12 paper liners. Sift together the flour, baking powder, and salt into a large bowl. Stir in the sugar and pecans.

Place the eggs in a large pitcher or bowl and beat lightly, then beat in the buttermilk, maple syrup, and oil. Make a well in the center of the dry ingredients and pour in the beaten liquid ingredients. Stir gently until just combined; do not overmix. Spoon the batter into the paper liners and top each muffin with a pecan half.

Bake in the preheated oven for 20 minutes, or until well risen, golden brown, and firm to the touch. Let cool in the pan for 5 minutes, then brush the tops with the maple syrup to glaze. Serve warm or transfer to a wire rack to cool completely.

111 *With maple crunch topping*

Omit the pecans from the top. Chop 1 cup pecans and mix with 3 tablespoons of brown sugar and 2 tablespoons of maple syrup, then spoon over the muffins before baking.

112 *Lemon cornmeal muffins*

Makes 12

6 tbsp sunflower oil, plus extra for greasing
4 lemons
about 3 tbsp low-fat plain yogurt
1¼ cups all-purpose flour
1 tbsp baking powder
½ tsp baking soda
heaping 1¾ cups medium cornmeal
heaping ½ cup superfine sugar
2 eggs

Preheat the oven to 400°F/200°C. Grease a 12-hole muffin pan. Finely grate the rind from the lemons and squeeze the juice. Add enough yogurt to make the juice up to a heaping 1 cup, then stir in the lemon rind.

Sift the flour, baking powder, and baking soda into a large bowl. Stir in the cornmeal and sugar. Place the eggs in a large pitcher or bowl and beat lightly, then beat in the oil. Make a well in the center of the dry ingredients and pour in the beaten liquid ingredients with the lemon and yogurt mixture. Stir gently until just combined; do not overmix. Spoon the batter into the muffin pan.

Bake in the preheated oven for 20 minutes, or until well risen, golden brown, and firm to the touch. Let cool in the pan for 5 minutes, then serve warm or transfer to a wire rack to cool completely.

113 *With Limoncello frosting*

Beat ⅔ cup mascarpone cheese, scant ½ cup confectioners' sugar, and 1 tablespoon of Limoncello liqueur together and spread over the cooled muffins. Scatter over chopped candied lemon peel.

114 Mini orange & cardamom muffins

MAKES 48

2 oranges
about 1⅓ cup milk
2 cups all-purpose flour
1 tbsp baking powder
pinch of salt
heaping ½ cup superfine sugar
6 cardamom pods, seeds removed and crushed
2 eggs
6 tbsp sunflower oil or 6 tbsp butter, melted and cooled

Preheat the oven to 400°F/200°C. Line two 24-hole mini muffin pans with 48 mini paper liners. Finely grate the rind from the oranges and squeeze the juice. Add enough milk to make the juice up to a generous 1 cup, then stir in the orange rind.

Sift together the flour, baking powder, and salt into a large bowl. Stir in the sugar and crushed cardamom seeds. Place the eggs in a pitcher and beat lightly, then beat in the orange and milk mixture and the oil. Make a well in the center of the dry ingredients and pour in the beaten liquid ingredients. Stir gently until just combined; do not overmix. Spoon the batter into the paper liners. Bake in the preheated oven for 15 minutes, or until well risen, golden brown, and firm to the touch. Let cool in the pans for 5 minutes, then serve warm or transfer to a wire rack to cool completely.

115 With white chocolate icing

Place 5½ oz/150 g white chocolate in a heatproof bowl, set the bowl over a saucepan of simmering water, and heat until melted. Stir in ½ teaspoon of orange flower water and drizzle over the muffins.

116 Mint chocolate chip muffins

MAKES 12

2 cups all-purpose flour
1 tbsp baking powder
pinch of salt
heaping ½ cup superfine sugar
scant 1 cup semisweet chocolate chips
2 eggs
generous 1 cup milk
6 tbsp sunflower oil or 6 tbsp butter, melted and cooled
1 tsp peppermint extract
1–2 drops of green food coloring (optional)
confectioners' sugar, for dusting

Preheat the oven to 400°F/200°C. Line a 12-hole muffin pan with 12 paper liners.

Sift together the flour, baking powder, and salt into a large bowl, then stir in the superfine sugar and chocolate chips. Place the eggs in a large pitcher or bowl and beat lightly, then beat in the milk, oil, and peppermint extract. Add 1–2 drops of food coloring, if using.

Make a well in the center of the dry ingredients and pour in the beaten liquid ingredients. Stir gently until just combined; do not overmix. Spoon the batter into the paper liners.

Bake in the preheated oven for 20 minutes, or until well risen and firm to the touch. Let cool in the pan for 5 minutes, then serve warm or transfer to a wire rack to cool completely. Dust with a little sifted confectioners' sugar before serving.

117 With chocolate ganache

Heat ¾ cup heavy cream in a saucepan until simmering, then pour over 6 oz/175 g chopped semisweet chocolate and stir until smooth. Cool and chill until thick, then spread over the muffins.

118 Moist gingerbread muffins

MAKES 12

6 tbsp sunflower oil or 6 tbsp butter, melted and cooled, plus extra for greasing
2 cups all-purpose flour
1 tbsp baking powder
4 tsp ground ginger
1½ tsp ground cinnamon
pinch of salt
heaping ½ cup light brown sugar
3 pieces preserved ginger in syrup, finely chopped
2 eggs
¾ cup milk
4 tbsp dark corn syrup

Preheat the oven to 400°F/200°C. Grease a 12-hole muffin pan. Sift together the flour, baking powder, ginger, cinnamon, and salt into a large bowl. Stir in the sugar and preserved ginger.

Place the eggs in a large pitcher or bowl and beat lightly, then beat in the milk, oil, and corn syrup. Make a well in the center of the dry ingredients and pour in the beaten liquid ingredients. Stir gently until just combined; do not overmix. Spoon the batter into the muffin pan.

Bake in the preheated oven for 20 minutes, or until well risen, golden brown, and firm to the touch. Let cool in the pan for 5 minutes, then serve warm or transfer to a wire rack to cool completely.

119 With lemon icing

Sift 1⅓ cups confectioners' sugar into a bowl, add 1 tablespoon of lemon juice, and mix until smooth, then spread over the muffins and let set.

120 Moist orange & almond muffins

MAKES 12

2 oranges
about ⅓ cup milk
1⅔ cups all-purpose flour
1 tbsp baking powder
pinch of salt
heaping ½ cup superfine sugar
⅔ cup ground almonds
2 eggs
6 tbsp sunflower oil or 6 tbsp butter, melted and cooled
½ tsp almond extract
scant ¼ cup raw brown sugar

Preheat the oven to 400°F/200°C. Line a 12-hole muffin pan with 12 paper liners. Finely grate the rind from the oranges and squeeze the juice. Add enough milk to make the juice up to a generous 1 cup, then stir in the orange rind. Sift together the flour, baking powder, and salt into a large bowl. Stir in the superfine sugar and ground almonds.

Place the eggs in a bowl and beat lightly, then beat in the orange mixture, oil, and almond extract. Make a well in the center of the dry ingredients, pour in the liquid ingredients, and mix. Spoon the batter into the paper liners. Sprinkle the raw brown sugar over the tops.

Bake in the preheated oven for 20 minutes, or until well risen, golden brown, and firm to the touch. Let cool in the pan for 5 minutes, then serve warm or transfer to a wire rack to cool completely.

121 With slivered almond topping

Scatter 1 cup slivered almonds over the muffins before they are baked.

122 Orange, walnut & rosemary muffins

MAKES 12

2 cups all-purpose flour
1 tbsp baking powder
½ tsp baking soda
pinch of salt
heaping ½ cup superfine sugar
½ cup walnuts, coarsely chopped
2 eggs
heaping 1 cup plain yogurt
6 tbsp sunflower oil or 6 tbsp butter, melted and cooled
finely grated rind of 2 oranges
1 tbsp finely chopped fresh rosemary leaves, plus extra sprigs for decorating

ICING
1½ cups confectioners' sugar
3–4 tsp fresh orange juice
finely grated rind of ½ orange

Preheat the oven to 400°F/200°C. Line a 12-hole muffin pan with 12 paper liners. Sift together the flour, baking powder, baking soda, and salt into a large bowl. Stir in the superfine sugar and walnuts.

Place the eggs in a large pitcher or bowl then beat in the yogurt, oil, orange rind, and chopped rosemary leaves. Make a well in the center of the dry ingredients and pour in the beaten liquid ingredients. Stir gently until just combined; do not overmix. Spoon the batter into the paper liners.

Bake in the preheated oven for 20 minutes, or until well risen, golden brown, and firm to the touch. Let cool in the pan for 5 minutes, then transfer to a wire rack to cool completely.

When the muffins are cold, make the icing. Sift the confectioners' sugar into a bowl. Add the orange juice and orange rind and stir until the mixture is smooth and thick enough to coat the back of a wooden spoon.

Spoon the icing on top of each muffin. Decorate with a rosemary sprig and let set for about 30 minutes before serving.

123 Marbled chocolate muffins

MAKES 12

6 tbsp sunflower oil or 6 tbsp butter, melted and cooled, plus extra for greasing
2 cups all-purpose flour
1 tbsp baking powder
pinch of salt
heaping ½ cup superfine sugar
2 eggs
generous 1 cup milk
1 tsp vanilla extract
2 tbsp unsweetened cocoa

Preheat the oven to 400°F/200°C. Grease a 12-hole muffin pan. Sift together the flour, baking powder, and salt into a large bowl. Stir in the sugar.

Place the eggs in a large pitcher or bowl and beat lightly, then beat in the milk, oil, and vanilla extract. Make a well in the center of the dry ingredients and pour in the beaten liquid ingredients. Stir gently until just combined; do not overmix.

Divide the batter between 2 bowls. Sift the cocoa into one bowl and mix together. Using teaspoons, spoon the batters into the muffin pan, alternating the chocolate batter and the plain batter.

Bake in the preheated oven for 20 minutes, or until well risen, golden brown, and firm to the touch. Let cool in the pan for 5 minutes, then serve warm or transfer to a wire rack to cool completely.

124 Marbled coffee muffins

Replace the cocoa with espresso coffee powder.

125 Springtime cupcakes

MAKES 24

⅔ cup butter, softened, or soft margarine
¾ cup superfine sugar
1 tsp vanilla extract
2 large eggs, lightly beaten
1 cup self-rising flour
heaping ¼ cup cornstarch

FOR DECORATING
4 oz/115 g ready-to-roll fondant
yellow and green food colorings
2⅔ cups confectioners' sugar
about 3 tbsp cold water
colored sprinkles

Preheat the oven to 375°F/190°C. Line two 12-hole muffin pans with 24 paper liners. Place the butter and sugar in a large bowl and beat together until light and fluffy, then beat in the vanilla extract. Gradually beat in the eggs. Sift in the flour and cornstarch and fold into the batter. Spoon the batter into the paper liners.

Bake in the preheated oven for 12–15 minutes, or until golden and springy to the touch. Transfer to a wire rack to cool completely.

To decorate, divide the fondant in half and color one half pale yellow. Roll out both halves, then use the sides of a round cookie cutter to cut out white and yellow petal shapes. Set aside.

Sift the confectioners' sugar into a bowl and mix with the water until smooth. Place half of the icing in a small pastry bag fitted with a small plain tip. Divide the remaining icing in half and color one portion yellow and the other green.

Cover 12 cakes with yellow icing and 12 with green icing. Arrange white petals on top of the yellow icing to form flowers. Pipe a little blob of white icing into the center of each flower, then add a few colored sprinkles on top of the white icing to form the center of the flower. Arrange the yellow petals on the green icing and decorate in the same way. Let set.

126 Flower & bug cupcakes

MAKES 12

1¼ cups self-rising flour
1 tsp baking powder
1 cup superfine sugar
¾ cup very soft butter, cut into small pieces
3 eggs
1 tsp vanilla extract
2 tbsp milk

FOR DECORATING
1¾ cups confectioners' sugar
1 tbsp lemon juice
1–2 tbsp water
few drops of blue and green food coloring
white chocolate disks
white chocolate rainbow disks
gummy bug candies

Preheat the oven to 350°F/180°C. Line a 12-hole muffin pan with 12 paper liners. Sift the flour, baking powder, and sugar into a bowl. Add the butter, eggs, vanilla extract, and milk and beat together until creamy. Spoon the batter into the paper liners. Bake in the preheated oven for 15–20 minutes, or until risen and golden. Transfer to a wire rack to cool.

Place the confectioners' sugar, lemon juice, and water in a bowl and mix together until smooth. Color half of the icing blue and half of the icing green. Spread the icing over the cakes. For flower cakes, place a white chocolate disk in the center and the rainbow ones around it. For bug cakes, pipe a leaf with green icing on each cake and top with a gummy worm or bug.

127 *Zoo animal cupcakes*

MAKES 9

¾ cup butter, softened, or soft margarine
1 cup superfine sugar
1 tsp vanilla extract
3 eggs, lightly beaten
⅔ cup dry unsweetened coconut
heaping 1 cup self-rising flour

FOR DECORATING
1½ tsp unsweetened cocoa
½ cup confectioners' sugar
about 10½ oz/300 g ready-to-roll fondant
food coloring, such as pink, yellow, brown, and black

Preheat the oven to 350°F/180°C. Line a 12-hole muffin pan with 9 paper liners. Place the butter and sugar in a large bowl and beat together until light and fluffy, then beat in the vanilla extract. Gradually beat in the eggs, then fold in the coconut and flour. Spoon the batter into the paper liners. Bake in the preheated oven for 20–25 minutes, or until golden and springy to the touch. Transfer to a wire rack to cool completely.

To decorate, sift the cocoa and confectioners' sugar into a small bowl and add enough cold water to form a smooth, thick icing. Spoon into a small pastry bag fitted with a writing tip. Leave a small piece of fondant white and color a small piece pink. Divide the remainder into 2 large pieces and one smaller piece. Color one large piece gray, using a small amount of black food coloring, and the other yellow, and the small piece brown.

To make the elephants, roll out the gray fondant and cut out 3 circles to fit the tops of the cake. To make the ears, cut out 6 circles and cut away one third of each circle. Roll out the pink fondant and cut out 6 smaller circles, then cut away one third of each circle. Place on top of the gray circles, pinch in the center and sides, and fix to the cakes with a little water. Roll a little gray fondant into a sausage shape to make the trunks and secure on the cakes with a little water. With a little white fondant, make the eyes and tusks and secure to the cake. Pipe the eyes and eyebrows with the cocoa icing.

To make the monkeys, roll and cut out 3 circles of brown fondant to fit the tops of the cake. Cut out the ears from brown fondant and make the centers of the ears with pink fondant. Secure to the cake by dampening with water. Cut out a circle of yellow fondant and cut out a small nick at the top, shape into the monkey's face, and secure to the cake. Make the eyes with a little white fondant and pipe on the remaining features.

To make the lions, cut out 3 circles of yellow fondant to fit the tops of the cake. Make the ears with brown and pink fondant and secure to the cakes. Make the nose with brown fondant and pipe on the features and the curly mane.

128 *Animal lovers' cupcakes*

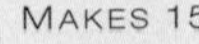

MAKES 15

⅓ cup golden raisins
grated rind and juice of ½ orange
8 tbsp butter, softened, or soft margarine
heaping ½ cup superfine sugar
½ tsp vanilla extract
2 eggs, lightly beaten
1¼ cups self-rising flour
¼ quantity buttercream (page 8)

FOR DECORATING
2¼ cups confectioners' sugar, sifted
2–3 tbsp orange juice
sugar animal cake decorations

Preheat the oven to 350°F/180°C. Line two 12-hole muffin pans with 15 paper liners. Place the golden raisins in a saucepan with the orange rind and juice and gently heat until almost boiling. Remove from the heat and let cool.

Place the butter and sugar in a large bowl and beat together until light and fluffy, then beat in the vanilla extract. Gradually beat in the eggs, then fold in the golden raisins and the juice. Sift in the flour and fold into the batter. Spoon the batter into the paper liners.

Bake in the preheated oven for 15–20 minutes, or until golden and springy to the touch. Transfer to a wire rack to cool completely.

To make the basic icing, sift the confectioners' sugar in a bowl and add enough orange juice to mix to a smooth coating consistency. Cover the cakes with the icing and let set.

To decorate, pipe a rosette of buttercream on the cakes and top with a sugar animal decoration.

129 Bling & buy cupcakes

MAKES 10

¾ cup butter, softened, or soft margarine
1 cup superfine sugar
1 tsp vanilla extract
3 eggs, lightly beaten
1¼ cups raspberries
1⅔ cups self-rising flour

FOR DECORATING
1 quantity buttercream (page 8)
pink, black, red, and yellow food coloring
2–3 oz/55–85 g ready-to-roll fondant
silver dragées
gummy candies

Preheat the oven to 350°F/180°C. Line a 12-hole muffin pan with 10 paper liners. Place the butter and sugar in a large bowl and beat together until light and fluffy, then beat in the vanilla extract.

Gradually beat in the eggs, then fold the raspberries and flour into the batter. Spoon the batter into the paper liners.

Bake in the preheated oven for 20–25 minutes, or until golden brown and springy to the touch. Transfer to a wire rack to cool completely.

To decorate, color the buttercream pale pink, then place in a pastry bag fitted with a large star tip and pipe the buttercream on top of the cakes.

Color the fondant and then mold into different shapes, such as handbags, high-heeled shoes, or rings. Arrange the shapes on the cupcakes, then press silver dragées into the frosting to form the handle of the bag and to decorate the shoes. Use gummy candies to make the gems on the rings.

130 Easy bling cupcakes

To save time, you can decorate the cakes with nonedible cake decorations: Look out for shoes, champagne bottles, or plastic rings and jewelry. Remember to remind people to remove them before eating. These would not be suitable to serve to young children.

131 Gooey chocolate & cream cheese cupcakes

MAKES 12

1¼ cups all-purpose flour
¼ cup unsweetened cocoa
¾ tsp baking soda
1 cup superfine sugar
¼ cup sunflower oil
¾ cup water
2 tsp white vinegar
½ tsp vanilla extract
⅔ cup soft cream cheese
1 egg, lightly beaten
heaping ½ cup semisweet chocolate chips

Preheat the oven to 350°F/180°C. Line a 12-hole muffin pan with 12 paper liners. Sift together the flour, cocoa, and baking soda into a large bowl. Stir ¾ cup of the sugar into the flour. Add the oil, water, vinegar, and vanilla extract and stir well together until combined.

Place the remaining sugar, cream cheese, and egg in a large bowl and beat together until well mixed. Stir in the chocolate chips.

Spoon the chocolate mixture into the paper liners and top each with a spoonful of the cream cheese mixture.

Bake in the preheated oven for 25 minutes, or until firm to the touch. Let the cupcakes cool in the pan for 10 minutes, then transfer to a wire rack to cool completely.

132 Lemon cheesecake cupcakes

MAKES 12

4½ tbsp butter
4½ oz/125 g graham crackers, crushed
½ cup superfine sugar
1¼ cups soft cream cheese
2 large eggs
finely grated rind of 1 large lemon
2 tsp lemon juice
½ cup sour cream
4 tbsp all-purpose flour
2 small lemons, sliced, for decorating

Preheat the oven to 325°F/160°C. Line a 12-hole muffin pan with 12 paper liners. Place the butter in a saucepan and heat gently until melted. Remove from the heat, then add the crushed graham crackers and 1 tablespoon of the sugar and mix well. Divide the cracker mixture among the paper liners and press down firmly with the back of a teaspoon. Chill in the refrigerator.

Meanwhile, place the remaining sugar, cream cheese, and eggs in a large bowl and beat together until smooth. Add the lemon rind and juice, and the sour cream and beat together until combined. Add the flour and beat well. Spoon the batter into the paper liners.

Bake in the preheated oven for 30 minutes, or until set but not browned. Let the cupcakes cool for 20 minutes, then transfer to a wire rack to cool completely.

When the cupcakes are cold, chill in the refrigerator for at least 3 hours. Decorate each cupcake with a twisted lemon slice.

133 Orange cheesecake cupcakes

Replace the lemon rind and juice with orange rind and juice, and decorate each cupcake with a twisted orange slice.

134 Easter cupcakes

MAKES 12

8 tbsp butter, softened, or soft margarine
heaping ½ cup superfine sugar
2 eggs, lightly beaten
⅔ cup self-rising flour
¼ cup unsweetened cocoa

TOPPING
6 tbsp butter, softened
1 cup confectioners' sugar
1 tbsp milk
2–3 drops vanilla extract
9 oz/260 mini sugar-coated chocolate eggs

Preheat the oven to 350°F/180°C. Line a 12-hole muffin pan with 12 paper liners.

Place the butter and sugar in a large bowl and beat together until light and fluffy, then gradually

beat in the eggs. Sift in the flour and cocoa and fold into the batter. Spoon the batter into the paper liners.

Bake in the preheated oven for 15–20 minutes, or until well risen and firm to the touch. Transfer to a wire rack to cool.

To make the buttercream topping, place the butter in a bowl and beat until fluffy. Sift in the confectioners' sugar and beat together until well mixed, adding the milk and vanilla extract.

When the cupcakes are cold, place the frosting in a pastry bag, fitted with a large star tip and pipe a circle around the edge of each cupcake to form a nest. Place chocolate eggs in the center of each nest to decorate.

135 Chocolate curl Easter cupcakes

Lightly sprinkle chocolate curls over the top and gently press into the buttercream topping around the edge of the cakes.

136 Really chocolatey Easter cupcakes

Add ½ cup chocolate chips to the cake batter. Top the cupcakes with chocolate buttercream (page 8) and press chocolate shavings into the frosting.

137 Christmas cupcakes

Makes 12

9 tbsp butter, softened
1 cup superfine sugar
4–6 drops almond extract
4 eggs, lightly beaten
1 heaping cup self-rising flour
½ cup ground almonds

TOPPING
1 lb/450 g white ready-to-roll fondant
2 oz/55 g green ready-to-roll colored fondant
1 oz/25 g red ready-to-roll colored fondant
confectioners' sugar, for dusting

Preheat the oven to 350°F/180°C. Line a 12-hole muffin pan with 12 paper liners. Place the butter, sugar, and almond extract in a large bowl and beat together until light and fluffy, then gradually beat in the eggs. Sift in the flour and fold into the batter, then fold in the ground almonds. Spoon the batter into the paper liners.

Bake in the preheated oven for 20 minutes, or until well risen, golden brown, and firm to the touch. Transfer to a wire rack to cool completely.

When the cupcakes are cold, knead the white fondant until pliable, then roll out on a surface lightly dusted with confectioners' sugar. Cut out 12 circles with a 2¾-inch/7-cm plain round cutter, rerolling the fondant as necessary. Place a circle on top of each cupcake.

Roll out the green fondant on a surface lightly dusted with confectioners' sugar. Using the palm of your hand, rub confectioners' sugar into the fondant to prevent it from spotting. Cut out 24 leaves with a holly leaf-shaped cutter, rerolling the fondant as necessary. Brush each leaf with a little cooled boiled water and place 2 leaves on top of each cupcake. Roll the red fondant between the palms of your hands to form 36 berries and place 3 in the center of the leaves on each cake to decorate.

138 Spicy Christmas cupcakes

Add 1 teaspoon of pumpkin pie spice to the cake batter. To decorate, cover the cakes with the white ready-to-roll fondant. Use green fondant to cut out Christmas tree shapes and use yellow fondant to make a star for the top of the trees.

139 Marzipan & fruit cupcakes

Add heaping ⅓ cup mixed dried fruit to the cake batter. To decorate, roll out some marzipan and cut out star shapes. Brush the tops of the cakes with a little warmed apricot jam and arrange marzipan stars on top.

140 Halloween cupcakes

Makes 12

8 tbsp butter, softened,
or soft margarine
heaping ½ cup superfine sugar
2 eggs
heaping ¾ cup self-rising flour

TOPPING
7 oz/200 g orange ready-to-roll
colored fondant
confectioners' sugar, for dusting
2 oz/55 g black ready-to-roll
colored fondant
tube of black decorating icing
tube of white decorating icing

Preheat the oven to 350°F/180°C. Line a 12-hole muffin pan with 12 paper liners. Place the butter, sugar, eggs, and flour in a large bowl and beat together until smooth. Spoon the batter into the paper liners.

Bake in the preheated oven for 15–20 minutes, or until well risen, golden, and firm to the touch. Transfer to a wire rack to cool.

When the cupcakes are cold, knead the orange fondant until pliable, then roll out on a surface dusted with confectioners' sugar. Rub confectioners' sugar into the fondant to prevent it from spotting. Cut out 12 circles with a 2¼-inch/5.5-cm round cutter, rerolling the fondant as necessary. Place a circle on top of each cake. Roll out the black fondant on a surface dusted with confectioners' sugar. Rub confectioners' sugar into the fondant to prevent it from spotting. Cut out 12 circles with a 1¼-inch/3-cm round cutter and place them in the center of the cakes. Using black decorating icing, pipe 8 legs onto each spider and draw eyes and a mouth with white decorating icing.

141 Pumpkin-decorated cupcakes

Cover the cakes with white fondant. Use orange fondant to cut out and make pumpkin shapes. Pipe on the stems of the pumpkins with green decorating icing and pipe a jagged mouth and eyes on the pumpkin with black decorating icing.

142 Spiderweb cupcakes

Melt 2 oz/55 g semisweet chocolate and spoon into a pastry bag fitted with a writing tip. Cover the cakes with basic icing (page 8). Pipe circles of chocolate onto the cakes and, using a skewer, quickly drag the chocolate from the center to the outside of the cakes several times to feather the icing and chocolate into a spiderweb design.

143 Valentine heart cupcakes

Makes 6

6 tbsp butter, softened,
or soft margarine
½ cup superfine sugar
½ tsp vanilla extract
2 eggs, lightly beaten
½ cup all-purpose flour
1 tbsp unsweetened cocoa
1 tsp baking powder

MARZIPAN HEARTS
confectioners' sugar, for dusting
1¼ oz/35 g marzipan
red food coloring (liquid or paste)

TOPPING
4 tbsp butter, softened
1 cup confectioners' sugar
1 oz/25 g semisweet chocolate, melted
6 chocolate flower decorations

To make the hearts, line a baking sheet with parchment paper and lightly dust with confectioners' sugar. Knead the marzipan until pliable, then add a few drops of red coloring and knead until evenly colored. Roll out the marzipan to a thickness of ¼ inch/5 mm on a surface dusted with confectioners' sugar. Cut out 6 hearts with a small heart-shaped cutter and place on the sheet. Leave for 3–4 hours.

To make the cupcakes, preheat the oven to 350°F/180°C. Line a 12-hole muffin pan with 6 paper liners. Place the butter, sugar, and vanilla extract in a large bowl and beat together until light and fluffy, then gradually beat in the eggs. Sift in the flour, cocoa, and baking powder and fold into the batter. Spoon the batter into the paper liners. Bake in the preheated oven for 20–25 minutes, or until well risen and firm to the touch. Transfer to a wire rack to cool completely.

To make the topping, place the butter in a bowl and beat until fluffy. Sift in the confectioners' sugar and beat until smooth. Add the melted chocolate and beat until mixed. Spread the frosting on top of each cake and decorate with a chocolate flower and a heart.

144 Cherry & vanilla heart cupcakes

Increase the vanilla extract to 1 teaspoon and the flour to ⅔ cup. Omit the cocoa and add ¼ cup quartered candied cherries. Decorate with vanilla buttercream instead of chocolate buttercream.

145 Gold & silver anniversary cupcakes

Makes 24

1 cup butter, softened
heaping 1 cup superfine sugar
1 tsp vanilla extract
4 large eggs, lightly beaten
1⅔ cups self-rising flour
5 tbsp milk

TOPPING
¾ cup butter
3 cups confectioners' sugar
silver or gold dragées

Preheat the oven to 350°F/180°C. Line two 12-hole muffin pans with 24 silver or gold foil cake liners. Place the butter, sugar, and vanilla extract in a large bowl and beat together until light and fluffy, then gradually beat in the eggs. Sift in the flour and fold into the mixture with the milk. Spoon the batter into the foil liners.

Bake in the preheated oven for 15–20 minutes, or until well risen and firm to the touch. Transfer to a wire rack to cool completely.

To make the topping, place the butter in a large bowl and beat until fluffy. Sift in the confectioners' sugar and beat together until well mixed. Place the topping in a pastry bag fitted with a medium star-shaped tip.

When the cupcakes are cold, pipe circles of frosting on top of each cake to cover the tops and sprinkle over the silver or gold dragées.

146 Ruby wedding cupcakes

Add 2 oz/55 g quartered candied cherries to the cake batter and decorate as before using red dragées.

147 Rocky mountain cupcakes

Makes 10

heaping ¾ cup butter, softened, or soft margarine
¾ cup superfine sugar
1 tsp vanilla extract
3 eggs, lightly beaten
heaping 1 cup self-rising flour
½ cup unsweetened cocoa

TOPPING
1 quantity chocolate buttercream (page 8)
3 oz/85 g mini marshmallows
½ cup walnuts, coarsely chopped
2 oz/55 g milk chocolate or semisweet chocolate, broken into pieces

Preheat the oven to 350°F/180°C. Line a 12-hole muffin pan with 10 paper liners. Place the butter and sugar in a large bowl and beat together until light and fluffy, then beat in the vanilla extract. Gradually beat in the eggs. Sift the flour and cocoa together and fold into the mixture. Spoon the batter into the paper liners.

Bake in the preheated oven for 20–25 minutes, or until golden and springy to the touch. Transfer to a wire rack to cool completely.

To decorate, pipe the buttercream on top of each cake to form a peak in the center. Mix the marshmallows and walnuts together and divide among the cakes, then press down lightly. Place the chocolate in a heatproof bowl, set the bowl over a pan of gently simmering water, and heat until melted. Drizzle over the tops of the cakes and let set.

148 Baby shower cupcakes with sugared almonds

MAKES 24

1¾ cups butter, softened
2 cups superfine sugar
finely grated rind of 2 lemons
8 eggs, lightly beaten
3 cups self-rising flour

TOPPING
3 cups confectioners' sugar
6–8 tsp hot water
red or blue food coloring (liquid or paste)
24 sugared almonds

Preheat the oven to 350°F/180°C. Line two 12-hole muffin pans with 24 paper liners. Place the butter, sugar, and lemon rind in a large bowl and beat together until light and fluffy, then gradually beat in the eggs. Sift in the flour and fold into the mixture. Spoon the batter into the paper liners.

Bake in the preheated oven for 20–25 minutes, or until well risen, golden brown, and firm to the touch. Transfer to a wire rack to cool.

When the cakes are cold, make the topping. Sift the confectioners' sugar into a bowl, add the hot water, and stir until smooth and thick enough to coat the back of a wooden spoon. Dip a skewer into the red or blue food coloring and stir it into the icing until it is evenly colored pink or pale blue. Spoon the icing on top of each cake. Top each with a sugared almond and let set for about 30 minutes.

149 Scented baby shower cupcakes

Omit the lemon rind and add 1 tablespoon of chopped lavender or rosemary to the cake batter after beating in the eggs. Decorate as before or with confetti-type sprinkles.

150 Chocolate brownie cupcakes

MAKES 12

8 oz/225 g semisweet chocolate, broken into pieces
6 tbsp butter
2 large eggs
1 cup dark brown sugar
1 tsp vanilla extract
1 cup all-purpose flour
¾ cup walnuts, chopped into small pieces

Preheat the oven to 350°F/180°C. Line a 12-hole muffin pan with 12 paper liners. Place the chocolate and butter in a saucepan and heat gently, stirring constantly, until melted. Remove from the heat and stir until smooth. Let cool slightly.

Place the eggs and sugar in a large bowl and whisk together, then add the vanilla extract. Stir in the flour until mixed together, then stir the melted chocolate into the mixture until combined. Stir in the chopped walnuts. Spoon the batter into the paper liners.

Bake in the preheated oven for 30 minutes, or until firm to the touch but still slightly moist in the center. Let the cupcakes cool for 10 minutes, then transfer to a wire rack to cool completely.

151 High-fiber muffins

Makes 12

4 cups high-fiber bran cereal
generous 1 cup skim milk
1 cup all-purpose flour
1 tbsp baking powder
1 tsp ground cinnamon
½ tsp freshly grated nutmeg
heaping ½ cup superfine sugar
⅔ cup raisins
2 eggs
6 tbsp sunflower oil

Preheat the oven to 400°F/200°C. Line a 12-hole muffin pan with 12 paper liners. Put the cereal and milk in a bowl and let soak for about 5 minutes, or until the cereal has softened.

Meanwhile, sift together the flour, baking powder, cinnamon, and nutmeg into a large bowl. Stir in the sugar and raisins.

Place the eggs in a large pitcher or bowl and beat lightly, then beat in the oil. Make a well in the center of the dry ingredients and pour in the beaten liquid ingredients and the cereal mixture. Stir gently until just combined; do not overmix. Spoon the batter into the paper liners.

Bake in the preheated oven for 20 minutes, or until well risen, golden brown, and firm to the touch. Let cool in the pan for 5 minutes, then serve warm or transfer to a wire rack to cool completely.

152 High-fiber seed muffins

Add 3 tablespoons of chopped mixed seeds, such as pumpkin, sunflower, and hemp seeds with the raisins.

153 Sunflower seed muffins

Makes 12

1 cup all-purpose flour
1 tbsp baking powder
heaping ½ cup light brown sugar
1⅔ cups rolled oats
heaping ½ cup golden raisins
½ cup sunflower seeds
2 eggs
generous 1 cup skim milk
6 tbsp sunflower oil
1 tsp vanilla extract

Preheat the oven to 400°F/200°C. Line a 12-hole muffin pan with 12 paper liners. Sift together the flour and baking powder into a large bowl. Stir in the sugar, oats, golden raisins, and scant ½ cup of the sunflower seeds.

Place the eggs in a large pitcher or bowl and beat lightly, then beat in the milk, oil, and vanilla extract. Make a well in the center of the dry ingredients and pour in the beaten liquid ingredients. Stir gently until just combined; do not overmix. Spoon the batter into the paper liners. Sprinkle the remaining sunflower seeds over the tops of the muffins.

Bake in the preheated oven for 20 minutes, or until well risen, golden brown, and firm to the touch. Let cool in the pan for 5 minutes, then serve warm or transfer to a wire rack to cool completely.

154 Muesli muffins

Makes 12

1 cup all-purpose flour
1 tbsp baking powder
heaping 1¾ cups unsweetened muesli
heaping ½ cup light brown sugar
2 eggs
generous 1 cup buttermilk
6 tbsp sunflower oil

Preheat the oven to 400°F/200°C. Line a 12-hole muffin pan with 12 paper liners. Sift together the flour and baking powder into a large bowl. Stir in the muesli and sugar.

Place the eggs in a large pitcher or bowl and beat lightly, then beat in the buttermilk and oil. Make a well in the center of the dry ingredients and pour in the beaten liquid ingredients. Stir gently until just combined; do not overmix. Spoon the batter into the paper liners.

Bake in the preheated oven for 20 minutes, or until well risen, golden brown, and firm to the touch. Let cool in the pan for 5 minutes, then serve warm or transfer to a wire rack to cool completely.

155 Apple & muesli muffins

Add heaping ¼ cup chopped dried apple to the muffin batter and add a dried apple ring to the top of each muffin before baking.

156 Wheat germ, banana & pumpkin seed muffins

Makes 12

6 tbsp sunflower oil, plus extra for greasing
1 cup all-purpose flour
1 tbsp baking powder
heaping ½ cup superfine sugar
1¼ cups wheat germ
⅓ cup pumpkin seeds
2 bananas
about ⅔ cup skim milk
2 eggs

Preheat the oven to 400°F/200°C. Grease a 12-hole muffin pan. Sift together the flour and baking powder into a large bowl. Stir in the sugar, wheat germ, and ¼ cup of the pumpkin seeds. Mash the bananas and place in a pitcher, then add enough milk to make up the purée to a heaping 1 cup.

Place the eggs in a large pitcher or bowl and beat lightly, then beat in the banana and milk mixture and the oil. Make a well in the center of the dry ingredients and pour in the beaten liquid ingredients. Stir gently until just combined; do not overmix. Spoon the batter into the muffin pan. Sprinkle the remaining pumpkin seeds over the top.

Bake in the preheated oven for 20 minutes, or until well risen, golden brown, and firm to the touch. Let cool in the pan for 5 minutes, then serve warm or transfer to a wire rack to cool completely.

157 With crunchy topping

Chop 2 tablespoons of pumpkin seeds and 3 oz/85 g banana chips and mix with 2 tablespoons of soft brown sugar. Scatter over the muffins before baking.

158 Whole wheat banana muffins

MAKES 12

⅓ cup raisins
3 tbsp fresh orange juice
1 cup all-purpose flour
1 cup whole wheat flour
1 tbsp baking powder
heaping ½ cup superfine sugar
2 bananas
about ⅓ cup skim milk
2 eggs
6 tbsp sunflower oil
finely grated rind of 1 orange

Put the raisins in a bowl, add the orange juice, and let soak for 1 hour. Preheat the oven to 400°F/200°C. Line a 12-hole muffin pan with 12 paper liners.

Sift together both types of flour and the baking powder into a large bowl, adding any bran left in the strainer. Stir in the sugar.

Mash the bananas and place in a pitcher, then add enough milk to make up the purée to a heaping ¾ cup. Place the eggs in a large pitcher or bowl and beat lightly, then beat in the banana and milk mixture, oil, soaked raisins, and orange rind. Make a well in the center of the dry ingredients and pour in the beaten liquid ingredients. Stir gently until just combined; do not overmix. Spoon the batter into the paper liners.

Bake in the preheated oven for 20 minutes, or until well risen, golden brown, and firm to the touch. Let cool in the pan for 5 minutes, then serve warm or transfer to a wire rack to cool completely.

159 With banana topping

Mash 1 ripe banana with ½ teaspoon of lemon juice. Beat ⅔ cup cream cheese with 2 tablespoons of confectioners' sugar and mix in the banana, then spread over the muffins.

160 Yogurt & spice muffins

MAKES 12

1 cup whole wheat flour
1 cup all-purpose flour
1 tbsp baking powder
½ tsp baking soda
4 tsp apple pie spice
heaping ½ cup superfine sugar
½ cup mixed dried fruit
2 eggs
heaping 1 cup low-fat plain yogurt
6 tbsp sunflower oil

Preheat the oven to 400°F/200°C. Line a 12-hole muffin pan with 12 paper liners. Sift together both types of flour, the baking powder, baking soda, and apple pie spice into a large bowl, adding any bran left in the strainer. Stir in the sugar and dried fruit.

Place the eggs in a large pitcher or bowl and beat lightly, then beat in the yogurt and oil. Make a well in the center of the dry ingredients and pour in the beaten liquid ingredients. Stir gently until just combined; do not overmix. Spoon the batter into the paper liners.

Bake in the preheated oven for 20 minutes, or until well risen, golden brown, and firm to the touch. Let cool in the pan for 5 minutes, then serve warm or transfer to a wire rack to cool completely.

161 Vanilla & spice muffins

Omit the dried fruit and use vanilla yogurt and the seeds from a vanilla bean.

162 Three grain muffins

MAKES 12

6 tbsp sunflower oil, plus extra for greasing
½ cup whole wheat flour
½ cup all-purpose flour
1 tbsp baking powder
heaping ½ cup dark brown sugar
scant ½ cup medium cornmeal
scant 1 cup rolled oats
2 eggs
generous 1 cup buttermilk
1 tsp vanilla extract

Preheat the oven to 400°F/200°C. Grease a 12-hole muffin pan. Sift together the flours and the baking powder into a large bowl, adding any bran left in the strainer. Stir in the sugar, cornmeal, and oats.

Place the eggs in a large pitcher or bowl and beat lightly, then beat in the buttermilk, oil, and vanilla extract. Make a well in the center of the dry ingredients and pour in the beaten liquid ingredients. Stir gently until just combined; do not overmix. Spoon the batter into the muffin pan.

Bake in the preheated oven for 20 minutes, or until well risen, golden brown, and firm to the touch. Let cool in the pan for 5 minutes, then serve warm or transfer to a wire rack to cool completely.

163 Corn muffins

MAKES 12

6 tbsp sunflower oil or 6 tbsp butter, melted and cooled, plus extra for greasing
1¼ cups all-purpose flour
1 tbsp baking powder
pinch of salt
freshly ground black pepper
heaping 1 cup medium cornmeal
2 eggs
generous 1 cup milk
1 cup frozen corn kernels

Preheat the oven to 400°F/200°C. Grease a 12-hole muffin pan. Sift together the flour, baking powder, salt, and pepper to taste into a large bowl. Stir in the cornmeal.

Place the eggs in a large pitcher or bowl and beat lightly, then beat in the milk and oil. Make a well in the center of the dry ingredients, pour in the beaten liquid ingredients, and add the corn. Stir gently until just combined; do not overmix. Spoon the batter into the muffin pan.

Bake in the preheated oven for 20 minutes, or until well risen, golden brown, and firm to the touch. Let cool in the pan for 5 minutes, then serve warm or transfer to a wire rack to cool completely.

164 Cranberry & almond muffins

Makes 12

6 tbsp sunflower oil or 6 tbsp butter, melted and cooled, plus extra for greasing
1⅔ cups all-purpose flour
1 tbsp baking powder
pinch of salt
heaping ½ cup superfine sugar
heaping ½ cup ground almonds
2 eggs
generous 1 cup buttermilk
½ tsp almond extract
heaping ½ cup fresh or frozen cranberries
scant ¼ cup raw brown sugar
scant ½ cup slivered almonds

Preheat the oven to 400°F/200°C. Grease a 12-hole muffin pan. Sift together the flour, baking powder, and salt into a large bowl. Stir in the superfine sugar and ground almonds.

Place the eggs in a large pitcher or bowl and beat lightly, then beat in the buttermilk, oil, and almond extract. Make a well in the center of the dry ingredients, pour in the beaten liquid ingredients, and add the cranberries. Stir gently until just combined; do not overmix. Spoon the batter into the muffin pan. Sprinkle the raw brown sugar and slivered almonds over the tops of the muffins.

Bake in the preheated oven for 20 minutes, or until well risen, golden brown, and firm to the touch. Let cool in the pan for 5 minutes, then serve warm or transfer to a wire rack to cool completely.

165 With almond crunch topping

Chop the slivered almonds and mix with the raw brown sugar and 4 crushed amaretti cookies, then sprinkle the mixture over the top of the muffins before baking.

166 Fresh flower muffins

Makes 12

2 cups all-purpose flour
1 tbsp baking powder
pinch of salt
heaping ½ cup superfine sugar
2 eggs
generous 1 cup buttermilk
6 tbsp sunflower oil or 6 tbsp butter, melted and cooled
finely grated rind of 1 lemon

TOPPING
6 tbsp butter, softened
1½ cups confectioners' sugar
12 edible flower heads, such as lavender, nasturtiums, violets, primroses, or roses, for decorating

Preheat the oven to 400°F/200°C. Line a 12-hole muffin pan with 12 paper liners. Carefully wash the flower heads and let dry on paper towels.

Sift together the flour, baking powder, and salt into a large bowl. Stir in the sugar. Place the eggs in a large pitcher or bowl and beat lightly, then beat in the buttermilk, oil, and lemon rind. Make a well in the center of the dry ingredients and pour in the beaten liquid ingredients. Stir gently until just combined; do not overmix. Spoon the batter into the paper liners.

Bake in the preheated oven for 20 minutes, or until well risen, golden brown, and firm to the touch. Let cool in the pan for 5 minutes, then transfer to a wire rack to cool completely.

To make the frosting, place the butter in a large bowl and beat until fluffy. Sift in the confectioners' sugar and beat together until smooth, then place in a pastry bag fitted with a large star tip and pipe circles on top of each muffin. Just before serving, place a flower head on top for decorating.

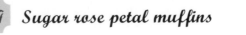

167 Sugar rose petal muffins

Brush 12 fresh rose petals with beaten egg white and dredge in superfine sugar, place on parchment paper to dry, and use for decorating the muffins.

168 Fresh orange muffins

MAKES 12

6 tbsp sunflower oil, plus extra for greasing
5 oranges
1 cup whole wheat flour
1 cup all-purpose flour
1 tbsp baking powder
heaping ½ cup superfine sugar
2 eggs
generous 1 cup fresh orange juice

Preheat the oven to 400°F/200°C. Grease a 12-hole muffin pan. Grate the rind from 2 of the oranges and set aside. Remove the peel from all of the oranges, discarding the white pith. Cut the flesh into segments, reserving 6 segments. Cut the reserved segments in half and set aside. Cut the remaining segments into small pieces.

Sift together both types of flour and the baking powder into a large bowl, adding any bran left in the strainer. Stir in the sugar.

Place the eggs in a large pitcher or bowl and beat lightly, then beat in the orange juice, oil, and reserved orange rind.

Make a well in the center of the dry ingredients, pour in the beaten liquid ingredients, and add the chopped oranges. Stir until combined; do not overmix. Spoon the batter into the muffin pan. Place the halved orange segments on the top.

Bake in the preheated oven for 20 minutes, or until well risen, golden brown, and firm to the touch. Cool for 5 minutes, then serve warm or transfer to a wire rack to cool completely.

169 Fresh peach muffins

Pit and peel 5 fresh peaches and proceed as for the oranges. Replace the orange juice with peach nectar.

170 Fresh strawberry & cream muffins

MAKES 12

6 tbsp sunflower oil or 6 tbsp butter, melted and cooled, plus extra for greasing
1 cup strawberries
2 cups all-purpose flour
1 tbsp baking powder
pinch of salt
heaping ½ cup superfine sugar
2 eggs
generous 1 cup light cream
1 tsp vanilla extract

TOPPING
½ cup heavy cream
12 whole small strawberries, for decorating

Preheat the oven to 400°F/200°C. Grease a 12-hole muffin pan. Chop the strawberries into small pieces. Sift together the flour, baking powder, and salt into a large bowl. Stir in the sugar and chopped strawberries.

Place the eggs in a large pitcher or bowl and lightly beat, then beat in the light cream, oil, and vanilla extract. Make a well in the center of the dry ingredients and pour in the beaten liquid ingredients.

Stir gently until just combined; do not overmix. Spoon the batter into the muffin pan.

Bake in the preheated oven for 20 minutes until well risen, golden brown, and firm to the touch. Let cool in the pan for 5 minutes, then transfer to a wire rack to cool completely.

Place the heavy cream in a bowl and whip until stiff. When the muffins are cold, pipe or spread the cream on top of each muffin, then top with a small strawberry.

171 With sweet wine & strawberry topping

Hull and slice the strawberries, pour over 2 tablespoons of sweet white wine, and let macerate for 10 minutes before spooning a few strawberry slices onto each muffin.

172 24-carrot gold cupcakes

Makes 12

¾ cup butter, softened, or soft margarine
heaping ½ cup superfine sugar
2 eggs, lightly beaten
heaping 1½ cup grated carrot
½ cup walnuts, finely chopped
2 tbsp orange juice
grated rind of ½ orange
1¼ cups self-rising flour
1 tsp ground cinnamon
12 walnut halves, for decorating

FROSTING
½ cup cream cheese
2 cups confectioners' sugar
1 tbsp orange juice

Preheat the oven to 350°F/180°C. Line a 12-hole muffin pan with 12 paper liners. Place the butter and sugar in a large bowl and beat together until light and fluffy, then gradually beat in the eggs. Fold in the grated carrot, walnuts, and orange juice and rind. Sift in the flour and cinnamon and fold into the batter until just combined. Spoon the batter into the paper liners.

Bake in the preheated oven for 15–20 minutes, or until golden and springy to the touch. Transfer to a wire rack to cool completely.

To make the frosting, place the cream cheese, confectioners' sugar, and orange juice in a bowl and beat together. Spread over the top of the cakes, then decorate with walnut halves.

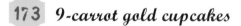

173 9-carrot gold cupcakes

Use ¾ cup grated carrot and ½ cup grated zucchini, and replace the walnuts with ⅓ cup golden raisins. Decorate the top of each cake with a pecan.

174 Pure indulgence almond cupcakes

Makes 12

7 tbsp butter, softened
½ cup superfine sugar
2 eggs, lightly beaten
¼ tsp almond extract
4 tbsp light cream
1¼ cups all-purpose flour
1½ tsp baking powder
¾ cup ground almonds

TOPPING
8 tbsp butter, softened
2 cups confectioners' sugar
few drops of almond extract
¼ cup toasted slivered almonds

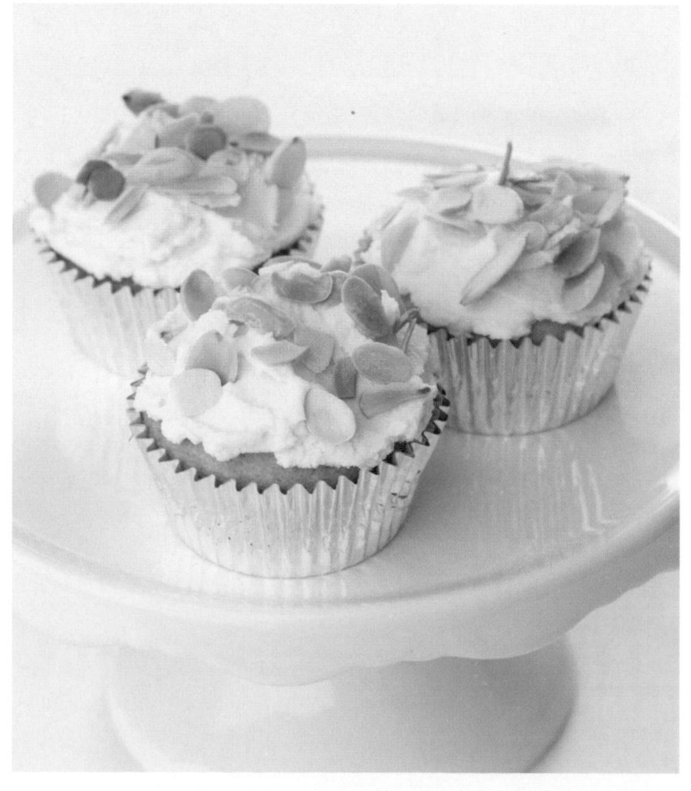

Preheat the oven to 350°F/180°C. Line a 12-hole muffin pan with 12 paper liners. Place the butter and sugar in a large bowl and beat together until light and fluffy. Gradually beat in the eggs, then add the almond extract and cream. Sift in the flour and baking powder and fold into the batter, then fold in the ground almonds. Spoon the batter into the paper liners.

Bake in the preheated oven for 25 minutes, or until golden brown and firm to the touch. Let the cupcakes cool in the pan for 10 minutes, then transfer to a wire rack to cool completely.

To make the frosting, place the butter in a large bowl and beat until creamy. Sift in the confectioners' sugar. Add the almond extract and beat until smooth. Spread the frosting on top of each cake, using a knife to form the frosting into swirls. Sprinkle the almonds over the top.

175 *Ice-cream cone cupcakes*

MAKES 8

¾ cup butter, softened, or soft margarine
1 cup superfine sugar
1 tsp vanilla extract
3 eggs, lightly beaten
⅔ cup ground almonds
heaping 1 cup self-rising flour

TOPPING
1 quantity buttercream (page 8)
8 mini chocolate bars
sugar sprinkles
seedless raspberry jam (optional)

Preheat the oven to 350°F/180°C. Line a 12-hole muffin pan with 8 paper liners. Place the butter and sugar in a large bowl and beat together until light and fluffy, then beat in the vanilla extract. Gradually beat in the eggs, then fold in the almonds and flour. Spoon the batter into the paper liners, peaking the batter slightly in the middle.

Bake in the preheated oven for 20–25 minutes, or until golden and springy to the touch. Transfer to a wire rack to cool completely.

Spoon the buttercream into a pastry bag fitted with a large star tip and pipe the frosting over the cakes to peak like an ice-cream cone. Press a chocolate bar into each cake and scatter a few sprinkles on top. Warm the raspberry jam and drizzle a little over each cake, if liked.

176 *Chocolate ice-cream cone cupcakes*

Replace 2 tablespoons of flour with cocoa. Decorate with chocolate buttercream (page 8), chocolate sprinkles, and a drizzle of chocolate sauce.

177 *Buttermilk & orange cupcakes*

MAKES 12

¾ cup dark brown sugar
heaping 1 cup butter, softened
2 eggs, lightly beaten
scant 1½ cups all-purpose flour
¾ tsp baking powder
½ tsp baking soda
½ cup buttermilk

FROSTING
2 cups confectioners' sugar
finely grated rind of 2 oranges, plus 1 tbsp juice

Preheat the oven to 350°F/180°C. Line a 12-hole muffin pan with 12 paper liners. Place the brown sugar and heaping ½ cup of the butter in a large bowl and beat together until light and fluffy, then gradually beat in the eggs. Sift in the flour, baking powder, and baking soda and fold into the batter, then fold in the buttermilk and grated orange rind of 1 orange. Spoon the batter into the paper liners.

Bake in the preheated oven for 30 minutes, or until firm to the touch. Let the cupcakes cool in the pan for 10 minutes, then transfer to a wire rack to cool completely.

To make the frosting, place the remaining butter in a large bowl and beat until fluffy. Sift in the confectioners' sugar. Add the remaining orange rind and the juice and beat together until smooth.

When the cupcakes are cold, spread the frosting on top, using a knife to form the frosting into swirls.

178 Lemon & raspberry cupcakes

MAKES 12

8 tbsp butter, softened
heaping ½ cup superfine sugar
2 eggs, lightly beaten
heaping ¾ cup self-rising flour
finely grated rind of 1 lemon
1 tbsp lemon curd
heaping ¾ cup fresh raspberries

TOPPING
2 tbsp butter
1 tbsp light brown sugar
1 tbsp ground almonds
1 tbsp all-purpose flour

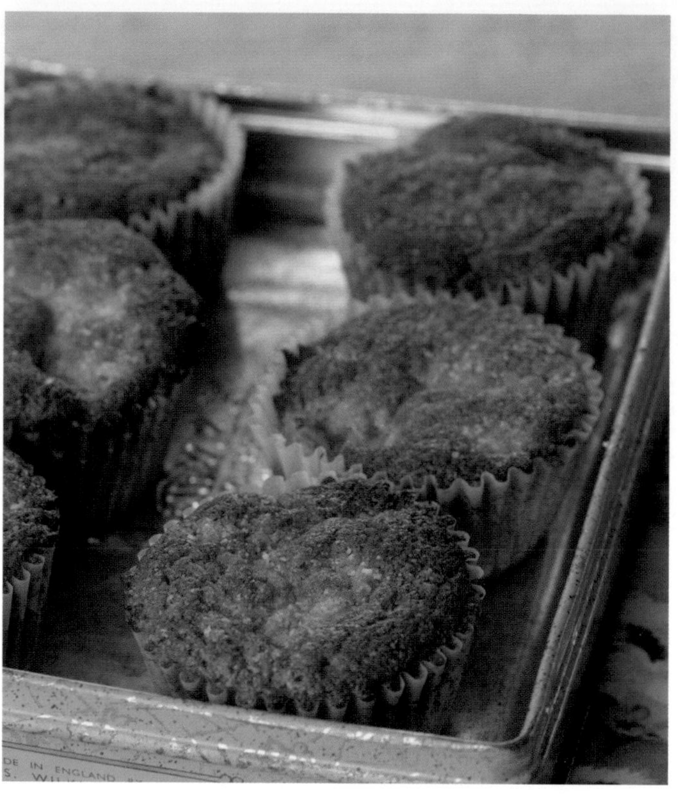

Preheat the oven to 400°F/200°C. Line a 12-hole muffin pan with 12 paper liners. To make the topping, place the butter in a saucepan and heat gently until melted. Pour into a bowl and add the sugar, ground almonds, and flour and stir together until combined.

To make the cupcakes, place the butter and sugar in a large bowl and beat together until light and fluffy, then gradually add the eggs. Sift in the flour and fold into the mixture. Fold in the lemon rind, lemon curd, and raspberries. Spoon the batter into the paper liners. Add the topping to cover the top of each cupcake and press down gently.

Bake in the preheated oven for 15–20 minutes, or until golden brown and firm to the touch. Let the cupcakes cool for 10 minutes, then transfer to a wire rack to cool completely.

179 Chocolate fruit & nut crispy cakes

MAKES 18

10½ oz/300 g semisweet chocolate, broken into pieces
heaping ⅔ cup butter, cut into cubes
¼ cup dark corn syrup
⅔ cup Brazil nuts, coarsely chopped
⅔ cup plumped dried raisins
7 cups cornflakes
18 candied cherries, for decorating

Place 18 paper liners on a baking sheet. Place the chocolate, butter, and dark corn syrup into a large saucepan and heat gently until the butter has melted and the ingredients are runny but not hot. Remove from the heat and stir until well mixed.

Add the chopped nuts and raisins to the pan and stir together until the fruit and nuts are covered in chocolate. Add the cornflakes and stir until combined.

Spoon the mixture evenly into the paper liners and top each with a candied cherry. Let set in a cool place for 2–4 hours before serving.

180 Devil's food cake with chocolate frosting

MAKES 18

3½ tbsp butter, softened, or soft margarine
heaping ½ cup dark brown sugar
2 large eggs
heaping ¾ cup all-purpose flour
½ tsp baking soda
¼ cup unsweetened cocoa
⅓ cup sour cream

FROSTING
4½ oz/125 g semisweet chocolate, broken into pieces
2 tbsp superfine sugar
⅔ cup sour cream

CHOCOLATE STICKS (optional)
3½ oz/100 g semisweet chocolate

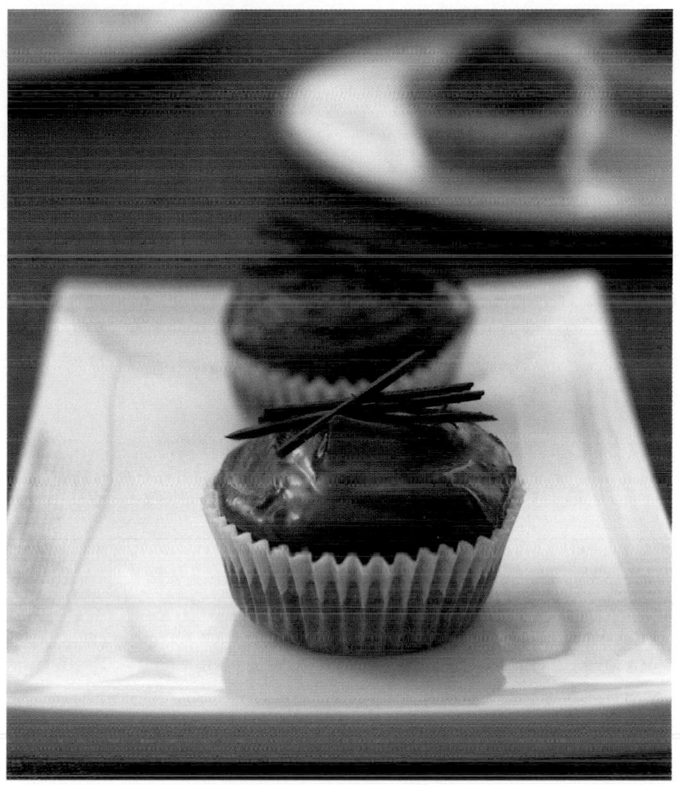

Preheat the oven to 350°F/180°C. Line two 12-hole muffin pans with 18 paper liners. Place the butter, sugar, eggs, flour, baking soda, and cocoa in a large bowl and beat together until just smooth. Fold in the sour cream. Spoon the batter into the paper liners.

Bake in the preheated oven for 20 minutes, or until well risen and firm to the touch. Transfer to a wire rack to cool completely.

To make the frosting, place the chocolate in a heatproof bowl, set the bowl over a saucepan of gently simmering water, and heat until melted. Let cool slightly, then whisk in the sugar and sour cream until combined. Spread the frosting over the tops of the cakes and let chill in the refrigerator before serving.

Decorate with chocolate sticks made by shaving semisweet chocolate with a vegetable peeler, if liked.

181 Strawberry shortcakes

MAKES 6

6 tbsp butter, plus extra for greasing
1⅔ cups self-rising flour, plus extra for dusting
½ tsp baking powder
½ cup superfine sugar
1 egg, lightly beaten
2–3 tbsp milk, plus extra for brushing

FILLING
1 tsp vanilla extract
heaping 1 cup mascarpone cheese
3 tbsp confectioners' sugar, plus extra for dusting
2¾ cups strawberries

Preheat the oven to 350°F/180°C. Lightly grease a large baking sheet. Sift the flour, baking powder, and sugar into a bowl. Add the butter and rub it in with your fingertips until the mixture resembles breadcrumbs.

Place the egg and 2 tablespoons of the milk in a bowl and beat together, then stir in the dry ingredients with a fork to form a soft, but not sticky, dough, adding more milk if necessary. Turn the dough out onto a lightly floured work surface and roll out to about ¾ inch/2 cm thick. Cut out rounds with a 2¾-inch/7-cm cookie cutter. Press the trimmings together and cut out more rounds until you have 6 rounds. Place the rounds on the baking sheet and brush with milk.

Bake in the preheated oven for 12–15 minutes, until firm and golden brown. Transfer to a wire rack to cool.

To make the filling, stir the vanilla extract into the mascarpone cheese with 2 tablespoons of the confectioners' sugar. Set aside a few whole strawberries, then slice the rest. Sprinkle with the remaining tablespoon of confectioners' sugar. Split the shortcakes in half horizontally.

Spoon half the mascarpone mixture onto the bases and top with sliced strawberries. Spoon over the remaining mascarpone mixture and cover with the tops. Dust with confectioners' sugar and top with the strawberries.

182 Raspberry shortcakes

Replace the strawberries with whole raspberries and sandwich with the mascarpone filling.

183 Chocolate muffins

Makes 12

1⅔ cups all-purpose flour
½ cup unsweetened cocoa
1 tbsp baking powder
pinch of salt
heaping ½ cup light brown sugar
2 eggs
heaping ¾ cup sour cream
6 tbsp sunflower oil or 6 tbsp butter, melted and cooled
3 tbsp dark corn syrup

Preheat the oven to 400°F/200°C. Line a 12-hole muffin pan with 12 paper liners. Sift together the flour, cocoa, baking powder, and salt into a large bowl. Stir in the sugar.

Place the eggs in a large pitcher or bowl and beat lightly, then beat in the sour cream, oil, and dark corn syrup. Make a well in the center of the dry ingredients and pour in the beaten liquid ingredients. Stir gently until just combined; do not overmix. Spoon the batter into the paper liners.

Bake in the preheated oven for 20 minutes, or until well risen and firm to the touch. Let cool in the pan for 5 minutes, then serve warm or transfer to a wire rack to cool completely.

184 Sticky toffee muffins

Makes 12

6 tbsp sunflower oil or 6 tbsp butter, melted and cooled, plus extra for greasing
scant 1½ cups pitted dates
generous 1 cup water
2 cups all-purpose flour
1 tbsp baking powder
pinch of salt
heaping ½ cup dark brown sugar
2 eggs
4 tbsp dulce de leche (from a jar), for serving

Preheat the oven to 400°F/200°C. Grease a 12-hole muffin pan. Put the dates and water in a food processor and blend to form a coarse purée. Sift together the flour, baking powder, and salt into a large bowl. Stir in the sugar.

Place the eggs in a large pitcher or bowl and beat lightly, then beat in the date purée and oil. Make a well in the center of the dry ingredients and pour in the beaten liquid ingredients. Stir gently until just combined; do not overmix. Spoon the batter into the muffin pan.

Bake in the preheated oven for 20 minutes, or until golden brown and firm to the touch. Let cool in the pan for 5 minutes, then serve warm or transfer to a wire rack to cool completely. Spread a teaspoon of dulce de leche over the top of each muffin before serving.

185 Toasted almond & apricot muffins

MAKES 12

heaping ½ cup dried apricots, cut into small pieces
3 tbsp fresh orange juice
⅓ cup blanched almonds
2 cups all-purpose flour
1 tbsp baking powder
pinch of salt
heaping ½ cup superfine sugar
2 eggs
generous ¾ cup buttermilk
6 tbsp sunflower oil or 6 tbsp butter, melted and cooled
¼ tsp almond extract
scant ½ cup slivered almonds

Place the apricots in a bowl, add the orange juice, and let soak for 1 hour.

Preheat the oven to 400°F/200°C. Line a 12-hole muffin pan with 12 paper liners. Preheat the broiler and line a broiler pan with foil. Spread out the almonds on the broiler pan and toast until golden, turning frequently. Cool then chop coarsely.

Sift together the flour, baking powder, and salt into a large bowl. Stir in the sugar and almonds.

Place the eggs in a large pitcher or bowl and beat lightly, then beat in the buttermilk, oil, and almond extract. Make a well in the center of the dry ingredients, pour in the beaten liquid ingredients, and add the soaked apricots. Stir gently until just combined; do not overmix. Spoon the batter into the paper liners. Scatter the slivered almonds on top of each muffin.

Bake in the preheated oven for 20 minutes, or until well risen, golden brown, and firm to the touch. Let cool in the pan for 5 minutes, then serve warm or transfer to a wire rack to cool completely.

186 With apricot centers

Fill each muffin liner halfway with batter and spoon in a little apricot preserve in the middle, then cover with the remaining batter.

187 Tropical banana & passion fruit muffins

MAKES 12

2 bananas
about ⅔ cup milk
2 cups all-purpose flour
1 tbsp baking powder
pinch of salt
heaping ½ cup light brown sugar
2 eggs
6 tbsp sunflower oil or 6 tbsp butter, melted and cooled
1 tsp vanilla extract
2 passion fruits
2 tbsp honey

Preheat the oven to 400°F/200°C. Line a 12-hole muffin pan with 12 paper liners. Mash the bananas and put in a pitcher. Add enough milk to make the purée up to a heaping 1 cup.

Sift together the flour, baking powder, and salt into a large bowl. Stir in the sugar.

Place the eggs in a large pitcher or bowl and beat lightly, then beat in the banana and milk mixture, oil, and vanilla extract. Make a well in the center of the dry ingredients and pour in the beaten liquid ingredients. Stir gently until just combined; do not overmix. Spoon the batter into the paper liners.

Bake in the preheated oven for 20 minutes, or until well risen, golden brown, and firm to the touch. Let cool in the pan for 5 minutes, then transfer to a wire rack to cool completely.

Meanwhile, halve the passion fruits and spoon the pulp into a small saucepan. Add the honey and heat very gently until warmed through. Spoon on top of the muffins before serving.

188 *Malted chocolate muffins*

MAKES 12

6 tbsp sunflower oil or 6 tbsp butter, melted and cooled, plus extra for greasing
5½ oz/150 g malted chocolate balls
1⅔ cups all-purpose flour
½ cup unsweetened cocoa
1 tbsp baking powder
pinch of salt
heaping ½ cup light brown sugar
2 eggs
generous 1 cup buttermilk

FROSTING
2 oz/55 g semisweet chocolate, broken into pieces
8 tbsp butter, softened
2 cups confectioners' sugar

Preheat the oven to 400°F/200°C. Grease a 12-hole muffin pan. Coarsely crush the chocolate balls, reserving 12 whole ones for decorating. Sift together the flour, cocoa, baking powder, and salt into a large bowl. Stir in the brown sugar and the crushed chocolate balls.

Place the eggs in a large pitcher or bowl and beat lightly, then beat in the buttermilk and oil. Make a well in the center of the dry ingredients and pour in the beaten liquid ingredients. Stir gently until just combined; do not overmix. Spoon the batter into the muffin pan.

Bake in the preheated oven for 20 minutes, or until well risen and firm to the touch. Let cool in the pan for 5 minutes, then transfer to a wire rack to cool completely.

To make the frosting, place the chocolate in a heatproof bowl, set the bowl over a saucepan of gently simmering water, and heat until melted. Remove from the heat. Place the butter in a large bowl and beat until fluffy. Sift in the confectioners' sugar and beat together until smooth and creamy. Add the melted chocolate and beat together. Spread the frosting on top of the muffins and decorate each with one of the reserved chocolate balls.

189 *Glazed honey muffins*

MAKES 12

6 tbsp sunflower oil, plus extra for greasing
1 cup whole wheat flour
1 cup all-purpose flour
1 tbsp baking powder
½ tsp baking soda
½ tsp pumpkin pie spice
¼ cup light brown sugar
heaping ½ cup golden raisins
2 eggs
heaping ¾ cup low-fat plain yogurt
8 tbsp honey

Preheat the oven to 400°F/200°C. Grease a 12-hole muffin pan. Sift together both flours, the baking powder, baking soda, and pumpkin pie spice into a large bowl, adding any bran left in the strainer. Stir in the sugar and golden raisins.

Place the eggs in a large pitcher or bowl and beat lightly, then beat in the yogurt, oil, and 4 tablespoons of the honey. Make a well in the center of the dry ingredients and pour in the beaten liquid ingredients. Stir until combined but do not overmix. Spoon the batter into the muffin pan.

Bake in the preheated oven for 20 minutes, or until well risen, golden brown, and firm to the touch. Let cool in the pan for 5 minutes, then drizzle 1 teaspoon of the remaining honey on top of each muffin. Serve warm or transfer to a wire rack to cool completely.

190 Carrot cake muffins

MAKES 12

6 tbsp sunflower oil, plus extra for greasing
2 cups all-purpose flour
1 tbsp baking powder
1 tsp pumpkin pie spice
pinch of salt
heaping ½ cup dark brown sugar
heaping 1 cup grated carrot
⅓ cup walnuts or pecans, coarsely chopped
⅓ cup golden raisins
2 eggs
¾ cup milk
finely grated rind and juice of 1 orange
strips of orange zest, for decorating

FROSTING
⅓ cup soft cream cheese
3 tbsp butter
⅓ cup confectioners' sugar

Preheat the oven to 400°F/200°C. Grease a 12-hole muffin pan. Sift together the flour, baking powder, pumpkin pie spice, and salt into a large bowl. Stir in the brown sugar, carrot, walnuts, and golden raisins.

Place the eggs in a large pitcher or bowl and beat lightly, then beat in the milk, oil, orange rind, and orange juice. Make a well in the center of the dry ingredients and pour in the beaten liquid ingredients. Stir gently until just combined; do not overmix. Spoon the batter into the muffin pan.

Bake in the preheated oven for 20 minutes, or until well risen, golden brown, and firm to the touch. Let cool in the pan for 5 minutes, then transfer to a wire rack to cool completely.

To make the frosting, place the cream cheese and butter in a bowl and sift in the confectioners' sugar. Beat together until light and fluffy. When the muffins are cold, spread the frosting on top of each, then decorate with strips of orange zest. Chill the muffins in the refrigerator until ready to serve.

191 With carrot decoration

Cut 6 plumped dried apricots in half and roll lengthwise to form a carrot shape, place on each muffin and add green "stalks" with pieces of angelica.

192 Goocy butterscotch cream muffins

MAKES 12

5½ oz/150 g hard butterscotch candies
2 cups all-purpose flour
1 tbsp baking powder
pinch of salt
heaping ½ cup dark brown sugar
2 eggs
generous 1 cup heavy cream
6 tbsp sunflower oil or 6 tbsp butter, melted and cooled

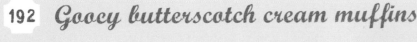

Preheat the oven to 400°F/200°C. Line a 12-hole muffin pan with 12 paper liners. Place the butterscotch candies in a strong plastic bag and hit with a meat mallet or the end of a wooden rolling pin until finely crushed.

Sift together the flour, baking powder, and salt into a large bowl. Stir in the sugar and crushed candies.

Place the eggs in a large pitcher or bowl and beat lightly, then beat in the cream and oil. Make a well in the center of the dry ingredients and pour in the beaten liquid ingredients. Stir gently until just combined; do not overmix. Spoon the batter into the paper liners.

Bake in the preheated oven for 20 minutes, or until well risen, golden brown, and firm to the touch. Let cool in the pan for 5 minutes, then serve warm or transfer to a wire rack to cool completely.

193 With butterscotch topping

Whip ¾ cup heavy cream with ½ teaspoon of vanilla extract, spread over the muffins, and scatter over 3 oz/85 g crushed butterscotch candies.

194 After-dinner coffee liqueur muffins

MAKES 12

2 tbsp instant coffee granules
2 tbsp boiling water
2 cups all-purpose flour
1 tbsp baking powder
pinch of salt
heaping ½ cup light brown sugar
2 eggs
generous ⅓ cup milk
6 tbsp sunflower oil or 6 tbsp butter, melted and cooled
6 tbsp coffee liqueur
scant ¼ cup raw brown sugar

Preheat the oven to 400°F/200°C. Line a 12-hole muffin pan with 12 paper liners. Put the coffee granules and boiling water in a cup and stir until dissolved. Let cool.

Meanwhile, sift together the flour, baking powder, and salt into a large bowl. Stir in the brown sugar. Place the eggs in a large pitcher or bowl and beat lightly, then beat in the milk, oil, dissolved coffee, and liqueur. Make a well in the center of the dry ingredients and pour in the beaten liquid ingredients. Stir gently until just combined; do not overmix. Spoon the batter into the paper liners. Sprinkle the raw brown sugar over the tops.

Bake in the preheated oven for 20 minutes, or until well risen, golden brown, and firm to the touch. Let cool in the pan for 5 minutes, then serve warm or transfer to a wire rack to cool completely.

195 With espresso icing

Sift 1 cup confectioners' sugar into a bowl, mix 1 teaspoon of espresso coffee powder with 1 tablespoon of boiling water, and add to the confectioners' sugar, then mix until smooth and spoon over the muffins.

196 Mocha muffins

MAKES 12

1⅔ cups all-purpose flour
1 tbsp baking powder
2 tbsp unsweetened cocoa
pinch of salt
8 tbsp butter, melted
¾ cup raw brown sugar
1 large egg, lightly beaten
½ cup milk
1 tsp almond extract
2 tbsp strong coffee
1 tbsp instant coffee powder
⅓ cup semisweet chocolate chips
scant ¼ cup raisins

COCOA TOPPING
3 tbsp raw brown sugar
1 tbsp unsweetened cocoa
1 tsp allspice

Preheat the oven to 375°F/190°C. Line a 12-hole muffin pan with 12 muffin paper liners. Sift the flour, baking powder, cocoa, and salt into a large bowl.

Place the butter and raw brown sugar in a separate bowl and beat together until light and fluffy, then stir in the beaten egg. Pour in the milk, almond extract, and coffee, then add the coffee powder, chocolate chips, and raisins and gently mix together.

Add the raisin mixture to the flour mixture and stir together until just combined. Do not overmix. Spoon the batter into the paper liners.

To make the topping, place the raw brown sugar in a bowl, add the cocoa and allspice, and mix together well, then sprinkle the topping over the muffins.

Bake in the preheated oven for 20 minutes, or until well risen and golden brown. Let cool in the pan for 5 minutes, then serve warm or transfer to a wire rack to cool completely.

197 With molten chocolate filling

Omit the raisins from the batter; you will need 3½ oz/100 g semisweet chocolate chips to make the centers. Spoon half the batter into each muffin paper and add a few chocolate chips to the middle, then top with the remaining batter and bake as before.

198 Spiced chocolate muffins

MAKES 12

7 tbsp butter, softened
¾ cup superfine sugar
heaping ½ cup light brown sugar
2 large eggs
⅔ cup sour cream
5 tbsp milk
heaping 1¾ cups all-purpose flour
1 tsp baking soda
2 tbsp unsweetened cocoa
1 tsp allspice
scant 1¼ cups semisweet chocolate chips

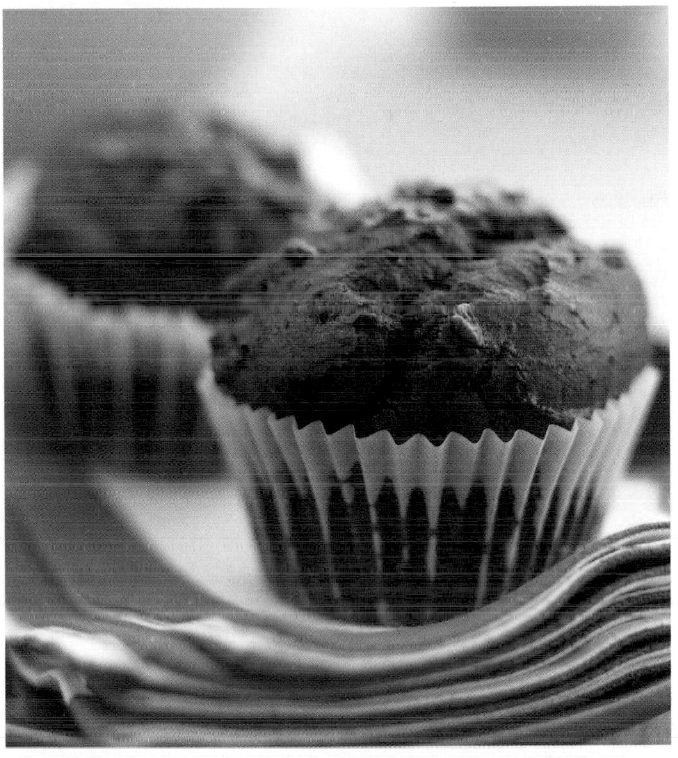

Preheat the oven to 375°F/190°C. Line a 12-hole muffin pan with 12 paper liners. Place the butter, superfine sugar, and brown sugar in a large bowl and beat together, then beat in the eggs, sour cream, and milk until thoroughly mixed.

Sift the flour, baking soda, cocoa, and allspice into a separate bowl and stir into the mixture. Add the chocolate chips and mix well. Spoon the batter into the paper liners.

Bake in the preheated oven for 25–30 minutes. Let cool in the pan for 10 minutes, then transfer to a wire rack to cool completely.

199 Rhubarb, ginger & raisin muffins

MAKES 12

9 oz/250 g rhubarb
9 tbsp butter, melted and cooled
generous ⅓ cup milk
2 eggs, lightly beaten
scant ½ cup all-purpose flour
2 tsp baking powder
⅔ cup superfine sugar
3 tbsp raisins
3 pieces preserved ginger, chopped

Preheat the oven to 375°F/190°C. Line a 12-hole muffin pan with 12 paper liners. Chop the rhubarb into lengths of about ½ inch/1 cm. Pour the melted butter and milk into a large bowl and beat in the eggs. Sift the flour and baking powder together and lightly fold into the wet mixture with the sugar. Gently stir in the rhubarb, raisins, and preserved ginger. Spoon the batter into the paper liners.

Bake in the preheated oven for 15–20 minutes, or until the muffins are risen and golden and spring back when gently touched in the center with the tip of an index finger. Let cool in the pan for 5 minutes, then serve warm.

200 With yogurt frosting

Stir 1 tablespoon of ginger syrup into ⅔ cup strained, whole-milk plain yogurt and spread over the warm muffins

Index